The **RHS** book of
Planting
Schemes

The **RHS** book of
Planting
Schemes

General Editor: Geoff Stebbings

conran
OCTOPUS

First published in 1999 by Conran Octopus Limited
37 Shelton Street, London WC2H 9HN
a part of Octopus Publishing Group
www.conran-octopus.co.uk

COMMISSIONING EDITOR: Stuart Cooper
EDITOR: Helen Woodhall
EDITORIAL ASSISTANT: Maxine McCaghy
ART EDITOR: Sue Storey
ILLUSTRATORS: Shirley Felts, Fiona Bell-Currie, Jeremy
Ford, Lynne Chadwick,
PICTURE RESEARCH: Claire Taylor
PRODUCTION: Oliver Jeffreys
INDEX: Helen Snaith

A catalogue record for this book is available from
the British Library

ISBN 1 84091 053 4

Colour origination by Sang Choy International, Singapore
Printed in China

CONTENTS

Page 1 *A restrained palette of yellow and white is given interest by the the contrasting textures and shapes of the plants.*
Page 2–3 *A backbone of hardy plants is fleshed out with tender cannas, castor oil plants and bananas to create a lush effect.*
Left *The statuesque shape of bearded iris makes them natural focal points in a garden border.*

INTRODUCTION

COMBINING PLANTS TO BEST EFFECT DEPENDS ON A SUCCESSFUL UNION OF ART AND SCIENCE. THE ELEMENT OF SCIENCE LIES IN RESEARCHING WHICH PLANTS GROW WELL TOGETHER AND WHICH SUIT THE CONDITIONS IN YOUR GARDEN. SOME GARDENERS LIKE THE CHALLENGE OF COAXING PLANTS WITH DIFFERENT REQUIREMENTS TO GROW IN THE SAME BORDER, BUT IT IS EASIER TO HAVE NATURE ON YOUR SIDE FROM THE START AND GROW PLANTS WHICH ARE SUITABLE FOR AND WILL THRIVE IN YOUR SOIL AND SITUATION. THE ART OF COMBINING PLANTS CONSISTS OF GROUPING THEM FOR AESTHETIC EFFECT. WITH SO MANY VARIABLES: FLOWERING TIME, GROWTH HABIT, TEXTURE, FOLIAGE AND HEIGHT, IT CAN BE HARD TO FIND THE RIGHT PLANT FOR A SCHEME.

BEFORE DECIDING ON A PLANTING SCHEME, YOU MUST THINK ABOUT THE EFFECT YOU WISH TO ACHIEVE. SOME PEOPLE WANT BORDERS TO LOOK GOOD IN A PARTICULAR SEASON OR WANT A CERTAIN COLOUR SCHEME. OTHERS, SUCH AS PLANT COLLECTORS, MAY FILL BORDERS WITH SIMILAR, BUT SUBTLY DIFFERENT, PLANTS.

A well-filled border will have colour and interest throughout its depth and height. Bulbs such as alliums help to give extra excitement.

Every plant has a unique beauty, but its placement in the garden can make the difference between a role as a starring soloist or a supporting player. Placing it as part of a harmonious scheme, where its neighbours have similar habit or colour, has a very different effect to placing it next to a plant which is totally different in appearance. The way to exaggerate the blue colouring of a flower is not to place it among other blues, but among flowers of the opposite side of the colour wheel – yellow. But a border filled solely with contrasts, whether of colour, form or texture, would be very jarring, and using similar colours is more restful. The extreme example of this is the monochrome or one-colour border, of which white is the most popular, perhaps because there are so many white flowers and so many of them are scented. Making a monochrome border is challenging because, by taking away colour, extra effort has to be taken to prevent the border looking boring. This means that greater emphasis is put on plant habit and size, leaves and texture.

Most plants are adaptable and will grow in a wide variety of soils and situations, but others have specific requirements, and it is unwise to combine plants with vastly different cultural needs. Moisture-loving plants may survive in dry soil but they will never thrive. Knowing which plants have similar cultural needs can also be helpful because those that grow together in the wild often complement each other in the garden.

When choosing plant neighbours, make sure that one of them is not a 'thug' that will swamp surrounding, more delicate, plants. If you are aware of the growth

There is more to grass than lawn: miscanthus and golden stipa make perfect companions to Crocosmia 'Bressingham Blaze'.

habits of a plant before you place it in a border at least you will be prepared to tackle the troublesome plant before it causes others damage.

No planting scheme can fulfil all expectations or desires, and it is best to concentrate on one or two functions in each planting. Setting a specific target can actually make plant choice easier because the choice of suitable plants is more limited. It is better to group plants with seasonal interest together rather than dot them around the garden, where late flowers in particular can be surrounded by dying foliage, spoiling the effect. Similarly, pots and containers can be placed together for maximum impact when they would be lost in the surrounding landscape when standing alone.

Bold clumps of grasses, blue delphiniums and purple alliums allow each to be appreciated in its own right within a border.

Skilful planting is also about getting the most out of your garden, and planting in layers using different types of plants with varied growing habits and flowering times is one way to get the maximum value from any area of garden. By planting spring-flowering bulbs among herbaceous plants, for example, the dying leaves of the bulbs are covered by fresh green foliage.

Creating a planting scheme is like creating a picture, and with so many colours and materials to use, this book can only hope to present a small number of the almost infinite number of possibilities.

BEDS AND BORDERS

FROM THE TRADITIONAL YEW-BACKED HERBACEOUS BORDER TO SMALL ISLAND BEDS SET IN A MANICURED LAWN, PLANTED AREAS CAN TAKE MANY FORMS. THE NATURE AND SIZE OF THE SITE WILL INFLUENCE THE PLANTING – ISLAND BEDS, FOR EXAMPLE, ARE DESIGNED TO BE VIEWED FROM ALL SIDES. IN GENERAL, THE LARGER THE BED THE TALLER THE PLANTS THAT CAN BE INCLUDED, BUT BY BREAKING THE RULES THE WHOLE CHARACTER OF THE GARDEN CAN BE CHANGED. SMALL BEDS, CRAMMED TOGETHER WITH NARROW PATHS BETWEEN, AND FILLED WITH LARGE-LEAVED, TOWERING PLANTS GIVE A JUNGLE-LIKE FEEL TO THE GARDEN. WIDEN THE PATHS AND PLANT THE BEDS WITH LOW-GROWING HEATHERS AND THE GARDEN OPENS UP AND BECOMES A MOORLAND.

Eryngium, achillea and helenium make bold contrasts of colour and texture in a herbaceous border at the height of summer.

COTTAGE BORDER

TRADITIONAL COTTAGE GARDENS combined flowers
and crops, and this border, in pastel pink and purple
shades, gives colour from summer through autumn
and provides flowers for cutting. This planting,
shown here in late summer, is suitable for most soils
including those over limestone and chalk. The
plants are hardy and trouble-free, so an exuberant
display is assured. Old-fashioned roses would be an
ideal complement, providing colour and perfume.

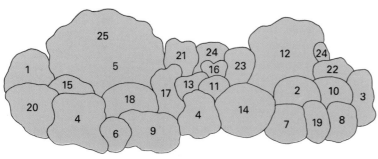

PLANTING GUIDE

1. *Anemone hupehensis* 'Hadspen Abundance'
2. *Artemisia* 'Powis Castle'
3. *Astrantia major* subsp. *involucrata* 'Shaggy'
4. *Astrantia major rubra*
5. *Clematis viticella*
6. *Diascia barberae* 'Ruby Field'
7. *Geranium* 'Ann Folkard'
8. *Geranium* x *oxonianum* 'Wargrave Pink'
9. *Geranium himalayense* 'Plenum'
10. *Gypsophila pacifica*
11. Kale 'Russian Red'
12. *Lavatera* 'Barnsley'
13. *Lythrum virgatum* 'The Rocket'
14. *Nepeta* 'Six Hills Giant'
15. *Penstemon* 'Sour Grapes'
16. *Phlox paniculata* 'Amethyst'
17. *Phlox paniculata* 'Sandringham'
18. *Salvia* x *superba*
19. *Salvia nemorosa* 'Ostfriesland'
20. *Sedum* 'Herbstfreude'
21. *Sidalcea* 'William Smith'
22. *Strobilanthes atropurpureus*
23. *Thalictrum delavayi*
24. *Verbena bonariensis*
25. *Viburnum rhytidophyllum*

ALTERNATIVE PLANTING

If a splash of autumn sun is more to your liking, try
a combination of bright yellows, lightened with
white and cream, and enriched with golds and tans.
Remember that the cottage garden look must have
a variety of plant types and the colour scheme
should not be too sophisticated or regular. Leave
gaps to fill with some summer and spring bedding
and do not forget tulips and daffodils.

BRIGHT SCHEME

1 *Solidago* 'Goldenmosa'

4 *Rudbeckia fulgida* var. *sullivantii* 'Goldsturm'

6 *Pilosella aurantiaca*

15 *Achillea millefolium* 'Paprika'

17 *Helenium* 'Moerheim Beauty'

18 *Salvia officinalis* 'Icterina'

20 *Sedum spectabile* 'Iceberg'

25 *Sambucus nigra* 'Madonna'

BORDER OF HOT COLOURS

ALTHOUGH THEY MIGHT APPEAR SIMPLE, borders with a limited
colour palette are a challenge to create, as the form, texture and shape
of the plants assume more importance. Use a wide range of
plant types to avoid a flat appearance. In a hot
border, purple foliage will enhance the scarlets
and crimsons and bright green foliage will
highlight the red blooms. This planting, shown
in late summer, suits most soils but the
levels of organic matter
must be maintained.

ALTERNATIVE PLANTING

Change this rich colour scheme into something
more fiery by adding copper and orange and
some yellow foliage. Golden conifers are useful
to provide year-round, bright colour and the fine
texture is ideal as a background for small flowers
like crocosmia and lobelia. Sunflowers are useful
to fill gaps in the early years and are available in
orange as well as yellow shades.

FIERY SCHEME

1. *Imperata cylindrica* 'Rubra'
2. *Heuchera* 'Chocolate Ruffles'
3. *Salvia officinalis* Purpurascens Group
7. *Lilium* 'Enchantment'
9. *Gaillardia* 'Dazzler'
11. *Spiraea japonica* 'Goldflame'
18. *Salpiglossis* 'Gloomy Rival' or 'Chocolate Pot'
21. *Physocarpus opulifolius* 'Diabolo'

PLANTING GUIDE

1. *Alchemilla mollis*
2. *Ajuga reptans* 'Atropurpurea'
3. *Berberis thunbergii* 'Atropurpurea Nana'
4. Ruby chard
5. *Cordyline australis* Purpurea Group
6. *Cotinus coggygria* 'Royal Purple'
7. *Crocosmia* 'Carmin Brillant' *or* 'Lucifer'
8. *Dahlia* 'Bishop of Llandaff'
9. *Euphorbia dulcis* 'Chameleon'
10. *Foeniculum vulgare* 'Purpureum'
11. *Fuchsia* 'Thalia'
12. *Heuchera micrantha* 'Palace Purple'
13. *Lobelia* 'Queen Victoria'
14. *Lobelia* 'Brightness'
15. *Lobelia* 'Dark Crusader'
16. *Macleaya cordata*
17. *Meconopsis cambrica flore-pleno*
18. *Nicotiana* Domino Series (red)
19. *Penstemon* 'Chester Scarlet'
20. *Ricinus communis* 'Impala'
21. *Rosa glauca*
22. *Verbena* 'Lawrence Johnston'

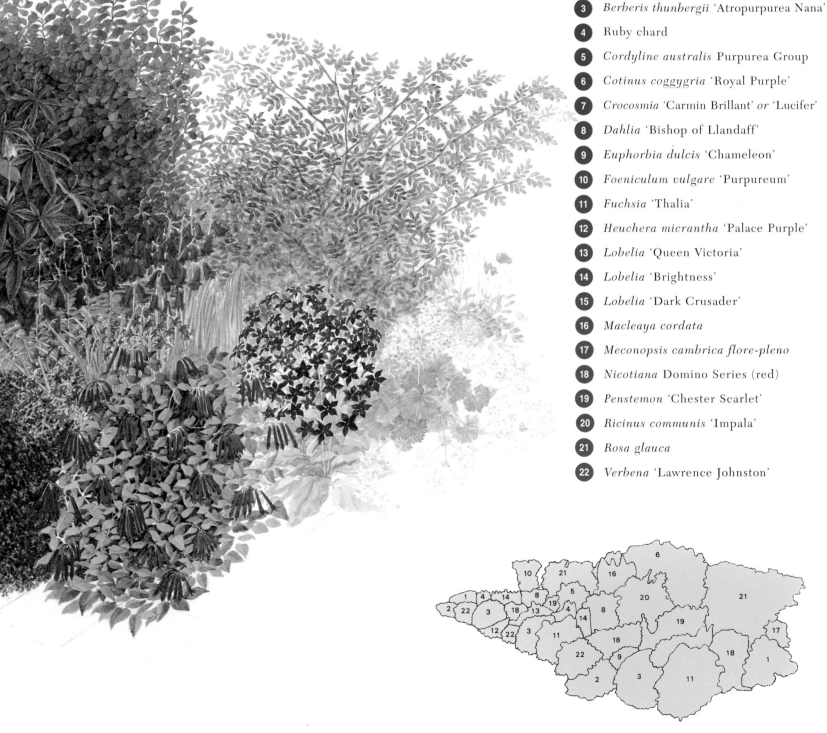

BORDER IN SOFT COLOURS

THIS PASTEL BORDER, shown here in midsummer, is filled with flowers, foliage and scents, and is ideal for dry soils in full sun. Most of the plants grow quite quickly and will rapidly cover the ground. With pinks, thymes, catmints and lilies, all this plan needs is a seat on which to relax.

The pale creams and white look particularly dramatic in the evening. If there is a wall behind the border, cover this with a climbing, scented rose such as 'Albertine' or 'New Dawn' or deliciously scented summer jasmine.

PLANTING GUIDE

1 *Achillea* 'Taygetea'

2 *Allium cristophii*

3 *Anaphalis triplinervis*

4 *Artemisia alba* 'Canescens'

5 *Artemisia* 'Powis Castle'

6 *Aster* x *frikartii* 'Mönch'

7 *Aster thomsonii* 'Nanus'

8 *Brachyglottis* (Dunedin Group) 'Sunshine'

9 *Calamintha nepeta*

10 *Dianthus* 'Doris', 'Fair Folly', 'Gran's Favourite', 'Musgrave's Pink'

11 *Euphorbia characias* subsp. *wulfenii*

12 *Fuchsia* 'Tom Thumb'

13 *Galtonia candicans*

14 *Gladiolus* 'The Bride'

15 *Hosta* (Tardiana Group) 'Halcyon'

16 *Iris pallida* subsp. *pallida*

17 *Iris pallida* 'Argentea Variegata'

18 *Kniphofia* 'Little Maid'

19 *Lilium regale*

20 *Limonium platyphyllum*

21 *Nerine bowdenii*

22 *Onopordum acanthium*

23 *Origanum laevigatum*

24 *Penstemon* 'Andenken an Friedrich Hahn'

25 *Penstemon* 'Evelyn'

26 *Perovskia* 'Blue Spire'

27 *Rosa* Margaret Merril

28 *Rosa* 'Mevrouw Nathalie Nypels'

29 *Sedum* 'Vera Jameson'

30 *Stachys byzantina*

31 *Thymus* x *citriodorus* 'Silver Queen'

32 *Verbena rigida*

33 *Verbena* 'Silver Anne'

34 *Verbena bonariensis*

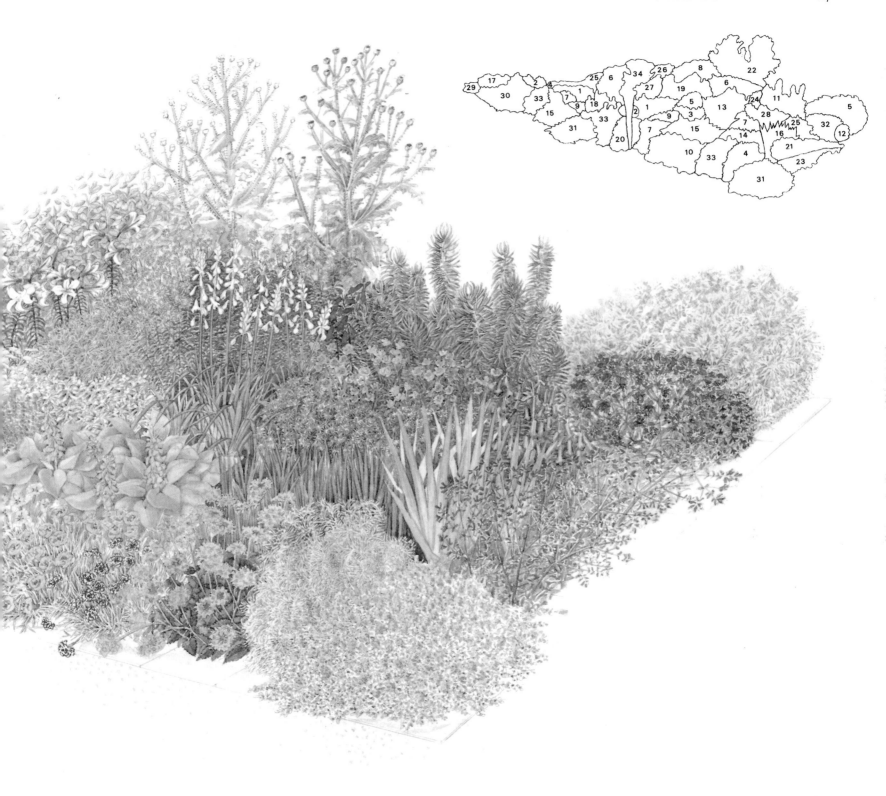

SMALL YELLOW SCHEME

YELLOW IS A BRIGHT AND CHEERFUL colour and reminiscent of spring. This scheme, shown here in mid- to late summer, uses clear flower colours and bright foliage. It must be regularly replenished with organic matter.

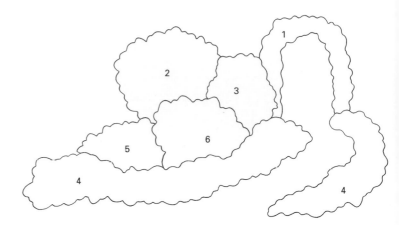

PLANTING GUIDE

1. *Achillea filipendulina* 'Gold Plate'
2. *Phalaris arundinacea* var. *picta* 'Feesey'
3. *Hemerocallis* 'Hyperion'
4. *Kniphofia* 'Ice Queen'
5. *Verbascum bombyciferum*
6. *Oenothera biennis*

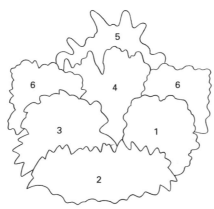

ORANGE BORDER

ORANGE FLOWERS AND FOLIAGE can be hard to place in the
garden without seeming garish, but in autumn their bright tones
are transformed by the low sun and look completely natural. This
scheme, shown here in mid- to late summer, combines colourful
foliage with the elegance of lilies, the tangy scents of houttuynia
and fennel, and a crop of blackberries. It is suitable for soil that
stays moist throughout the year and it must be regularly
replenished with organic matter. The curving path, with an arch
as its focus, encourages the visitor to explore.

PLANTING GUIDE

1 *Blackberry* 'Oregon Thornless'
2 *Sambucus nigra* 'Guincho Purple'
3 *Foeniculum vulgare* 'Purpureum'
4 *Houttuynia cordata* 'Chameleon'
5 *Mimulus cardinalis*
6 *Lilium lancifolium*

ALTERNATIVE PLANTING

If you want orange shades, or a brighter
colour range, earlier in the year, change the
fennel to a bright grass and the elder to a
golden buddleja. For more colourful edging
try *Houttuynia cordata* 'Flame', which has
bright foliage with wide cream markings.

SUMMER SCHEME

1 Tayberry
2 *Buddleja* x *weyeriana* 'Sungold'
3 *Miscanthus sinensis* 'Zebrinus'
4 *Houttuynia cordata* 'Flame'
5 *Ligularia dentata* 'Desdemona'
6 *Lilium* African Queen Group

TWO COLOURS FOR A SHADY BORDER

THIS BORDER FOR LIGHT SHADE, cast by a wall or a nearby but not overhanging tree and shown here in late summer, combines two blocks of colours with a linking group in the centre. On the left are plants from the blue spectrum with blue-green leaves and pink and mauve flowers. On the right are plants from the yellow spectrum with yellowish foliage and insignificant flowers. Hostas are particularly useful in this border because their leaf shape links the two parts but the colour range spans the blue and yellow parts of the spectrum. Their flowers add extra interest. If there is space the blocks of plants can be extended into long drifts which overlap and fill seasonal gaps in the border more effectively. This planting requires moist, well-drained soil.

ALTERNATIVE PLANTING

If you wish to increase the contrast between the blue and yellow ends of the border, retain the linking group and replace the pinker flowers with more lavender and blue. Deep purples look rich in sun but can be dull in shade so should be avoided unless they are set in front of bright foliage. Variegated forms of the existing plants can be substituted, or add bulbs such as daffodils and lilies.

BLUE SPECTRUM

1. *Amsonia tabernaemontana*
2. *Aconitum napellus*
3. *Hosta* 'Krossa Regal'

YELLOW SPECTRUM

8. *Miscanthus sinensis* 'Zebrinus'
9. *Valeriana phu* 'Aurea'
10. *Hosta* 'Sum and Substance'
11. *Lonicera nitida* 'Baggesen's Gold'

PLANTING GUIDE

BLUE SPECTRUM

1 *Anemone hupehensis* 'September Charm'

2 *Astilbe chinensis* var. *taquetii* 'Superba'

3 *Hosta sieboldiana* var. *elegans*

4 *Rosa glauca*

LINKING GROUP

5 *Hemerocallis* 'Marion Vaughn'

6 *Phlox paniculata*

7 *Hosta* 'Aureomarginata'

YELLOW SPECTRUM

8 *Nepeta govaniana*

9 *Alchemilla mollis*

10 *Hosta rohdeifolia* f. *albopicta*

11 *Osmanthus decorus*

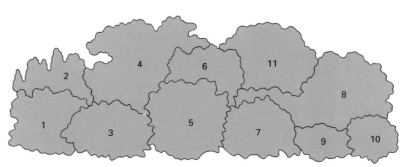

GREY AND PURPLE BORDER

THIS BORDER FOR DRY SOIL in a sunny spot, shown here
in late summer, is at its best in summer and
autumn, though many of the plants are
evergreen and look good throughout the
year. The grey and silver foliage
reflects the light, and purple
leaves develop their deepest
colouring in strong sunlight. In
the early years of the border's
development annuals such as
white cosmos, castor oil plants
and trailing *Helichrysum
petiolare* can be used to fill
gaps. Bulbs such as *Allium
cristophii*, purple gladioli and
galtonia can be added.

PLANTING GUIDE

1. *Berberis temolaica*
2. *Eryngium giganteum*
3. *Senecio cineraria* 'White Diamond'
4. *Foeniculum vulgare* 'Purpureum'
5. *Tanacetum densum* subsp. *amani*
6. *Salix exigua*
7. *Rosa glauca*

8. *Helichrysum splendidum*
9. *Iris pallida* 'Variegata'
10. *Sedum* 'Ruby Glow'
11. *Atriplex halimus*
12. *Berberis thunbergii* 'Rose Glow'
13. *Hebe pimeleoides* 'Quicksilver'
14. *Euphorbia myrsinites*

15. *Cynara cardunculus*
16. *Cotinus* 'Grace'
17. *Artemisia absinthium* 'Lambrook Silver'
18. *Helictotrichon sempervirens*
19. *Cupressus arizonica* var. *glabra*
20. *Buddleja fallowiana* var. *alba*
21. *Hebe* 'Red Edge'

ALTERNATIVE PLANTING

In a small garden this scheme can be repeated with smaller plants. If using *Eucalyptus gunnii*, cut back all side shoots to the main stem in spring annually to retain the juvenile foliage and prevent the plant becoming a large tree. The pittosporum can be pruned in spring or summer for cut foliage. This scheme is suitable for a small corner that gets sun all day, in poor soil.

SMALL-SCALE SCHEME

1 *Pittosporum tenuifolium* 'Atropurpureum'

2 *Eryngium bourgatii*

3 *Festuca glauca* 'Blaufuchs'

4 *Artemisia absinthium* 'Lambrook Silver'

5 *Acaena saccaticupula* 'Blue Haze'

6 *Eucalyptus gunnii*

7 *Artemisia lactiflora* Guizhou Group

8 *Salvia officinalis* Purpurascens Group

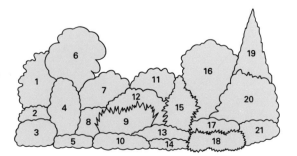

PALE COLOURS IN THE SHADOWS

IN THE EVENING and in semi-shade, pale flowers seem to glow against dark foliage, and this border for spring and early summer colour, shown here in late spring, is ideal for warm evenings. Place it against a dark green background such as a yew hedge or laurels. In dense shade some of these plants will struggle. This planting tolerates dryish soil in summer. Expect the groups to run and intermingle over the years.

PLANTING GUIDE

1 *Anemone narcissiflora*

2 *Convallaria majalis*

3 *Digitalis purpurea* f. *albiflora*

4 *Fritillaria meleagris alba*

5 *Tiarella cordifolia*

6 *Viola odorata* 'Alba'

7 *Corylus avellana*

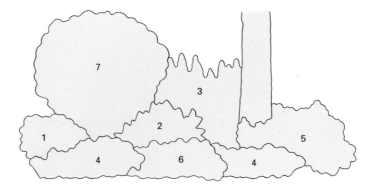

EXOTIC SCHEME

THE VICTORIANS WERE MASTERS of combining plants with bold foliage and exotic flowers to create subtropical bedding, but it is easy and fun to do with a combination of tender perennials and easily grown annuals. Choose bold, large leaves and bright flower colours. Cannas are essential, and there are many cultivars from which to choose, with larger, more exotic flowers than *Canna indica*. For extra colour pop in lilies and dahlias. This planting is shown in late summer and suits soil that does not dry out.

PLANTING GUIDE

1. *Alonsoa warscewiczii*
2. *Amaranthus caudatus* 'Viridis'
3. *Arundo donax*
4. *Canna indica* 'Purpurea'
5. *Eucomis bicolor*
6. *Hibiscus trionum*
7. *Melianthus major*
8. *Nicotiana langsdorffii*
9. *Nicotiana* 'Lime Green'
10. *Ricinus communis* 'Impala'
11. *Verbena* 'Lawrence Johnston'

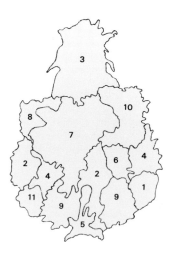

FIVE-INTO-ONE BORDER

THIS PLAN FOR A LARGE BORDER in a sunny place with
average soil combines five groups of plants that can be
used together to give colour throughout the year or
separately for particular seasons. The scheme, shown
here in early summer, suits dryish soil. Most of the
plants are deciduous and the border would benefit
from evergreen background such as conifers or a
wall. Each group combines shrubs and
herbaceous plants that are easy to grow and do
not require any special treatment. Most also
grow and establish quickly. Many of the edging
plants have a sprawling habit that is ideal for
softening the edges of paths and drives.

PLANTING GUIDE

A: Three shrubs to provide colour over
a long period with an ornamental grass
for contrast of form

1. *Kolkwitzia amabilis* 'Pink Cloud'
2. *Potentilla fruticosa* 'Abbotswood'
3. *Lavandula* 'Sawyers'
4. *Miscanthus sinensis* 'Variegatus'

B: A small group that will provide
interest in autumn

1. *Clerodendrum trichotomum*
2. *Ceanothus* x *delileanus* 'Topaze'
3. *Ballota pseudodictamnus*
4. *Liatris spicata* 'Kobold'

C: Berberis provides a strong accent
in this scented group for summer

1. *Cytisus battandieri*
2. *Berberis thunbergii* f. *atropurpurea*
3. *Rosa pimpinellifolia* double white
4. *Iris* 'Blue Shimmer'

D: A well-balanced group with interest
from spring through to autumn

1. *Cotoneaster franchetii*
2. *Prunus tenella* 'Fire Hill'
3. *Achillea* 'Moonshine'
4. *Salvia* x *sylvestris* 'Mainacht'

E: A combination of pastel-coloured
flowers and handsome foliage

1. *Lavatera* 'Barnsley'
2. *Perovskia* 'Blue Spire'
3. *Eryngium* x *tripartitum*
4. *Crambe maritima*

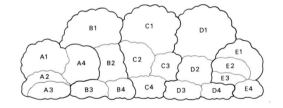

ALTERNATIVE PLANTING

For a similar scheme in shade, there are fewer
flowering plants from which to choose, but many
are evergreen. There are also fewer plants with
scented foliage because these tend to be provided
by herbs and grey-leaved plants. These alternative
suggestions will thrive in light or medium shade,
but establishing plants under trees is difficult
because of the competing roots and dense shade.

SCHEME FOR SHADE

B: **1** *Osmanthus heterophyllus* 'Variegatus'

2 *Aucuba japonica* 'Rozannie'

3 *Bergenia cordifolia* 'Purpurea'

4 *Iris foetidissima*

C: **1** *Clethra alnifolia*

2 *Photinia davidiana* 'Palette'

3 *Viburnum* x *burkwoodii*

4 *Hosta* 'Royal Standard'

AUTUMN COLOUR

The fleeting glories of autumn can be appreciated even in a small garden. This scheme brings together plants that are attractive all year but have a special beauty in autumn. It suits well-drained soil that doesn't dry out.

PLANTING GUIDE

1. *Pyracantha* 'Orange Glow'
2. *Vitis vinifera* 'Purpurea'
3. *Crocosmia* 'Firebird'
4. *Juniperus* x *pfitzeriana* Gold Sovereign
5. *Pleioblastus auricomus*
6. *Anthriscus sylvestris* 'Ravenswing'
7. *Dryopteris dilatata*
8. *Acer palmatum* 'Orido-Nishiki'
9. *Ophiopogon planiscapus* 'Nigrescens'
10. *Tolmiea menziesii* 'Taff's Gold'
11. *Hosta fortunei* var. *aureomarginata*
12. *Miscanthus sinensis* var. *purpurascens*
13. *Euonymus fortunei* 'Canadale Gold'
14. *Aster* x *frikartii* 'Mönch'

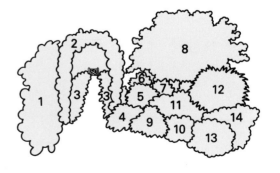

SPRING SCHEME

THE RAISED BED in this small garden is the focus of attention in spring. The bright yellow of many spring flowers makes a blue and yellow border a natural colour choice for this season. Spring bulbs can be grown in pots and tucked among existing plants or displayed in attractive containers. A touch of grey foliage contrasts with the fresh spring colours to complete the composition. This planting is suitable for soil over chalk or limestone.

PLANTING GUIDE

1. *Artemisia* 'Powis Castle'

2. *Rosa* Highfield

3. *Hosta* 'Bressingham Blue'

4. *Narcissus* 'February Gold'

5. *Juniperus squamata* 'Blue Carpet'

6. *Euonymus fortunei* 'Emerald 'n' Gold'

7. *Jasminum nudiflorum*

8. *Lonicera nitida* 'Baggesen's Gold'

9. *Gleditsia triacanthos* 'Sunburst'

10. *Elaeagnus* x *ebbingei* 'Limelight'

11. *Rosmarinus officinalis* 'Sissinghurst Blue'

12. *Forsythia* x *intermedia* 'Spring Glory'

13. *Pulmonaria angustifolia* 'Munstead Blue'

14. *Euphorbia polychroma* 'Major'

15. *Clematis alpina* 'Frances Rivis'

16. *Scilla siberica*

17. *Hedera helix* 'Sagittifolia Variegata'

18. **Pot on base:** *Scilla siberica* 'Spring Beauty', *Voila* x *wittrockiana* cultivars (pansy), *Hedera helix* 'Eva', *Primula vulgaris*

19. **Small flower pots:** *Crocus chrysanthus* 'Gipsy Girl', *Anemone blanda, Iris danfordiae, Narcissus* 'Golden Bells', *Crocus chrysanthus* 'Skyline'

LAYERS TO EXTEND THE SUMMER

IN SMALL GARDENS THE IDEA of planting in layers is especially
important because it is a way of getting the maximum number
of plants, and colour and interest from any area.
This scheme shown in late summer, for a small
corner, uses lilac to support a climbing
clematis, and to give shade for surrounding
plants. To extend the season of display
still further, bulbs and a hellebore are
planted for colour in winter and early
spring. This planting needs neutral to
acid soil that is rich in leafmould.

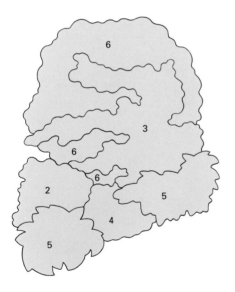

PLANTING GUIDE

1 *Athyrium niponicum* var. *pictum*

2 *Anemonopsis macrophylla*

3 *Clematis* 'Little Nell'

4 *Cyclamen hederifolium*

5 *Helleborus lividus*

6 *Lilium martagon* var. *cattaniae*

7 *Syringa vulgaris*

LAYERS TO GIVE COLOUR IN WINTER

THE GROUND UNDER DECIDUOUS SHRUBS is often bare in winter, and this space is wasted because there are many plants that will flourish and bring colour in late winter and spring. This scheme extends the season of colour into the spring once the yellow flowers of a witch hazel have faded. The shrub then provides support for a late-flowering clematis and shade for a host of plants that also enjoy moist, neutral soil.

PLANTING GUIDE

1 *Anemone nemorosa* 'Allenii'

2 *Cardamine raphanifolia*

3 *Clematis* 'Perle d'Azur'

4 *Corydalis ochroleuca*

5 *Hacquetia epipactis*

6 *Narcissus cyclamineus*

7 *Pulmonaria longiflora*

8 *Uvularia grandiflora*

9 *Hamamelis mollis*

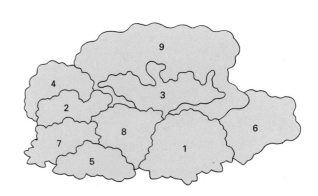

OLD-FASHIONED BORDER

ALTHOUGH GARDENERS HAVE A THIRST for novelties, many
of the most interesting plants are those that have been
grown for centuries. This midsummer border is planted
with some old-fashioned favourites. Many are not from far-
flung corners of the world, but are selections of native
plants, such as the rosulate form of the common plantain
with flower spikes like green roses. Others are rare
antiques that have been passed down through generations
of gardeners. This planting suits moist, well-drained soils.

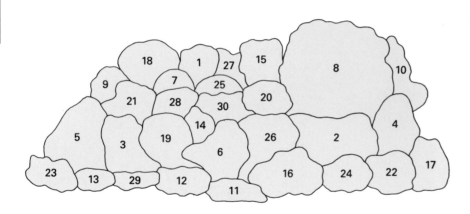

PLANTING GUIDE

1. *Anthemis tinctoria*
2. *Monarda didyma*
3. *Stachys officinalis*
4. *Erysimum cheiri* 'Bloody Warrior'
5. *Erysimum cheiri* 'Harpur Crewe'
6. *Dianthus caryophyllus*
7. *Cosmos astrosanguineus*
8. *Rosa rubiginosa*
9. *Rosmarinus officinalis* 'Aureus'
10. *Cynara cardunculus* Scolymus Group

11. *Lysimachia nummularia* 'Aurea'
12. *Viola tricolor*
13. *Bellis perennis* 'Prolifera'
14. *Hyoscyamus niger*
15. *Lilium candidum*
16. *Pulmonaria officinalis*
17. *Reseda odorata*
18. *Myrtus communis*
19. *Nepeta racemosa*
20. *Lavandula* x *intermedia* Dutch Group

21. *Iris* 'Florentina'
22. *Calendula officinalis*
23. *Plantago major* 'Rosularis'
24. *Rhodiola rosea*
25. *Ruta graveolens*
26. *Silene dioica* 'Flore Pleno'
27. *Sium sisarum*
28. *Hesperis matronalis*
29. *Fragaria vesca* 'Variegata'
30. *Valeriana officinalis*

ALTERNATIVE PLANTING

Many of the plants in the main scheme have a perfume, but this alternative includes other plants with fragrant leaves or flowers that would have been used to mask smells in the home, deter pests, clean wounds or flavour food. *Saponaria* (soapwort) was used to clean skin when rubbed to release the sap. They will grow in average soil and provide interest through the summer.

SCENTED SCHEME

3 *Acorus calamus* 'Variegatus'

5 *Saponaria officinalis* 'Rosea Plena'

9 *Tanacetum balsamita*

12 *Salvia officinalis*

13 *Mentha pulegium*

21 *Pulicaria dysenterica* (syn. *Inula dysenterica*)

23 *Galium odoratum*

29 *Prunella vulgaris*

LOW-MAINTENANCE SCHEME

IN A WILD AREA where plants can spread and intermingle, this border, shown in midsummer, will give a long season of colour. It tolerates most soils. The plants either spread through the soil or self-seed; the main work required will be to thin out vigorous plants and remove unwanted seedlings. Shrubs of golden elder and contorted hazel give interest in winter and summer, but the hazel is quite slow-growing and will need care when it is young. The elder will grow fast and can be cut back hard each spring to get the best leaf colour. In cold areas, the white argyranthemum and red lobelia will need protection in winter.

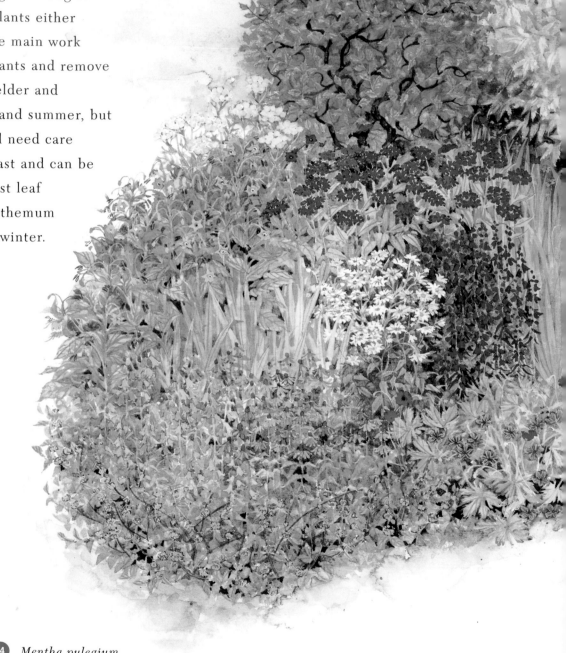

PLANTING GUIDE

1. *Argyranthemum foeniculaceum*
2. *Ranunculus acris* 'Flore Pleno'
3. *Borago officinalis*
4. *Echinacea pallida*
5. *Corylus avellana* 'Contorta'
6. *Papaver rhoeas*
7. *Geranium procurrens*
8. *Sambucus racemosa* 'Plumosa Aurea'
9. *Stachys sylvatica*
10. *Iris spuria*
11. *Iris versicolor*
12. *Lobelia* 'Queen Victoria'
13. *Lychnis chalcedonica*
14. *Mentha pulegium*
15. *Campanula rapunculus*
16. *Polygonatum* x *hybridum*
17. *Tanacetum vulgare* var. *crispum*

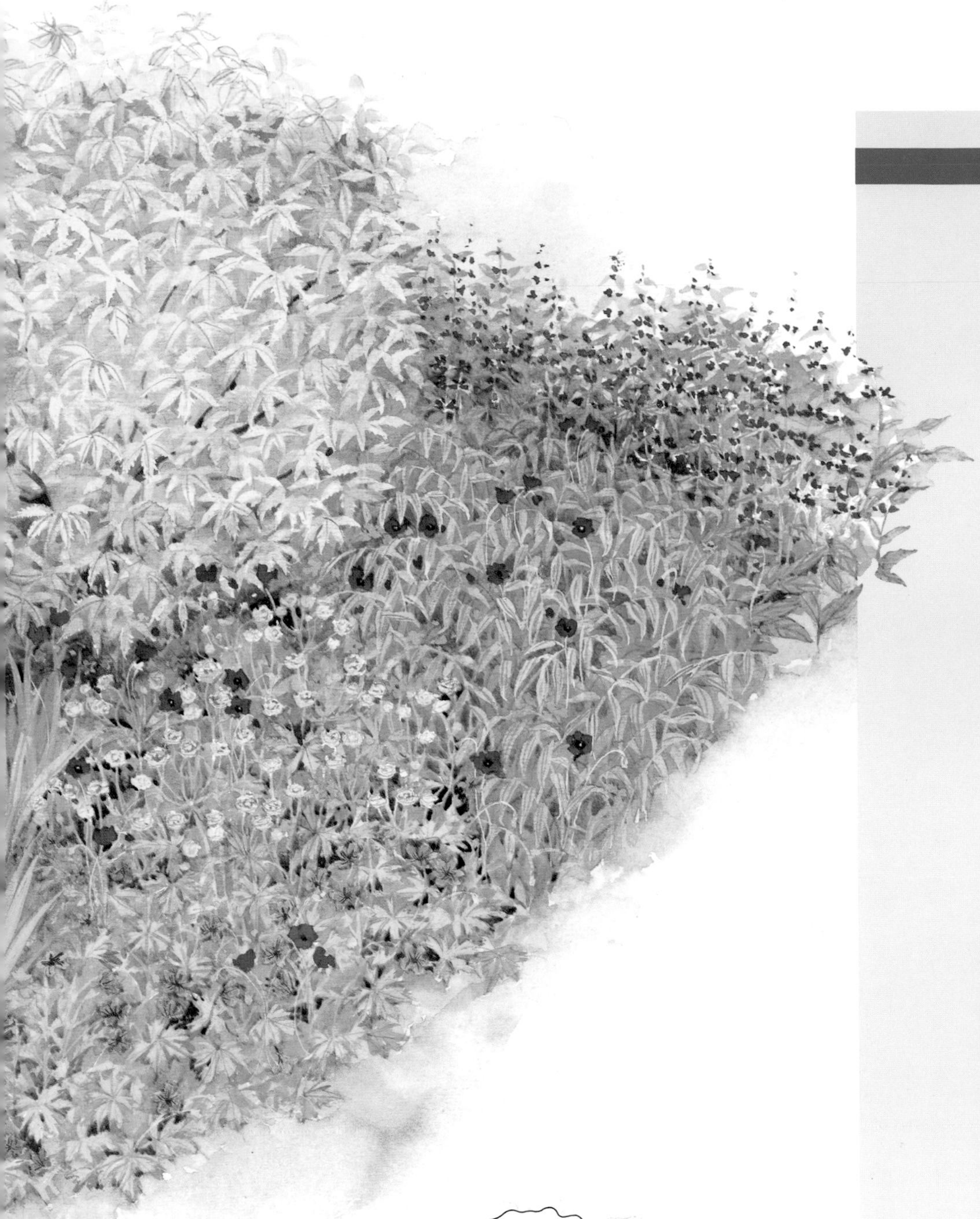

ALTERNATIVE PLANTING

This alternative planting scheme uses similar plants but with the addition of some extra golden foliage the planting is brighter, without making any extra work. The mix of corn marigolds (*Chrysanthemum segetum*) and pheasant's eye (*Adonis aestivalis*) is borrowed from the English countryside and they should self-seed. The variegated comfrey (*Symphytum*) makes a dense cover.

BRIGHTER SCHEME

- 2 *Adonis aestivalis*
- 6 *Chrysanthemum segetum*
- 7 *Geranium* 'Ann Folkard'
- 8 *Physocarpus opulifolius* 'Dart's Gold'
- 9 *Lamium orvala*
- 10 *Iris sibirica* 'Cambridge'
- 12 *Liatris spicata*
- 16 *Symphytum* 'Goldsmith'

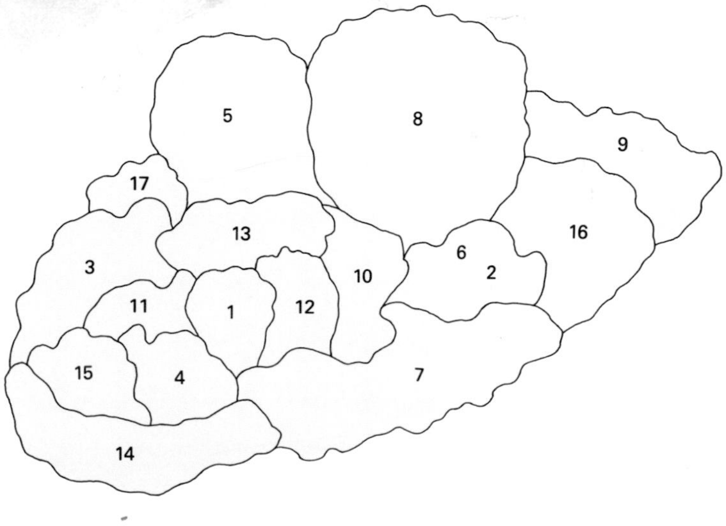

BED IN DRY SHADE

MOST GARDENERS HAVE TROUBLE planting
beds in dry shade, yet it is one of the
most common garden situations,
under trees or beside tall hedges.
Many plants thrive here, but they
often have small flowers. This border,
shown in late spring, includes a wide
range of plants; most have attractive
foliage and many are evergreen. Extra
interest can be added by planting
spring-flowering bulbs. The masses of
foliage will hide their dying leaves.

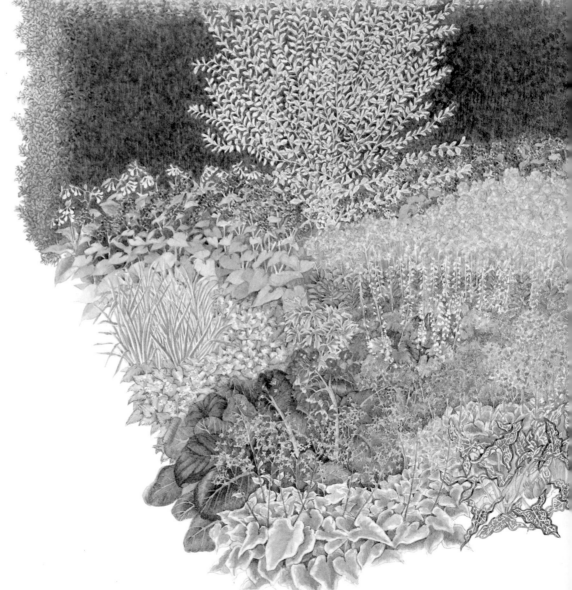

PLANTING GUIDE

1. *Anemone* x *hybrida* 'Honorine Jobert'
2. *Arum italicum*
3. *Bergenia* Ballawley Hybrids
4. *Bergenia* 'Silberlicht'
5. *Bergenia purpurascens*
6. *Brunnera macrophylla* 'Hadspen Cream'
7. *Brunnera macrophylla* Aluminium Spot
8. *Epimedium* x *versicolor* 'Neosulphureum'
9. *Euonymus fortunei* 'Emerald 'n' Gold'
10. *Euphorbia amygdaloides* var. *robbiae*
11. *Geranium macrorrhizum* 'Variegatum'
12. *Helleborus foetidus*
13. *Hosta lancifolia*
14. *Iris foetidissima*
15. *Iris foetidissima* 'Variegata'
16. *Ligustrum ovalifolium* 'Argenteum'
17. *Lunaria annua*
18. *Lunaria rediviva*
19. *Symphytum ibericum*
20. *Tanacetum parthenium* 'Aureum'
21. *Tellima grandiflora* Rubra Group
22. *Tolmiea menziesii* 'Taff's Gold'
23. *Valeriana phu* 'Aurea'

ALTERNATIVE PLANTING

White flowers and foliage are the best colours for shade, lighting up dark corners. Variegated plants are usually slower-growing than their green counterparts so this scheme, which relies on foliage and flowers, will require care in the early stages to ensure that the plants get off to a good start. By restricting the colour of flowers a cool effect, lightened by the fine leaves of ferns, can be created. This planting looks good in winter too, with very little bare ground, especially if variegated ivy is allowed to trail through.

VARIEGATED SCHEME

- ① *Geranium phaeum* 'Album'
- ② *Cyclamen hederifolium* f. *album*
- ③ *Geranium macrorrhizum* 'Album'
- ⑥ *Duchesna indica* 'Harlequin'
- ⑧ *Vinca minor* 'Alba Variegata'
- ⑪ *Dryopteris filix-mas*
- ⑮ *Liriope muscari*
- ⑰ *Lunaria annua* 'Alba Variegata'
- ⑲ *Polygonatum* x *hybridum*
- ㉑ *Hypericum androsaemum* 'Mrs Gladis Brabazon'

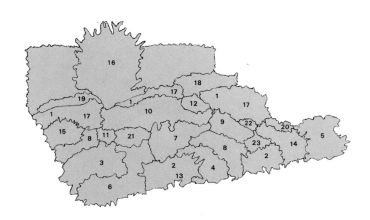

SEASIDE GARDEN

GARDENERS BY THE COAST have special problems to deal with. Strong winds can kill shoots and dry out leaves, salt spray can scorch growth, and soils are often thin or sandy. There are advantages, however. The sea protects coastal gardens from extreme cold, so exotic plants can be used that would be killed by frost in inland gardens. This border is designed to be planted with a windbreak of pines or tamarisk to protect it against the strongest winds, and is shown in summer. Most of the plants are evergreen and there is a strong contrast of foliage and plenty of flowers. A pebble mulch will prevent loss of soil moisture through evaporation and make a pleasant contrast to the sprawling nature of the plants in the front row.

PLANTING GUIDE

1 Hebe 'Midsummer Beauty'
2 Genista hispanica
3 Kniphofia 'Little Maid'
4 Artemisia 'Powis Castle'
5 Spartium junceum
6 Cistus x aguilarii 'Maculatus'
7 Bupleurum fruticosum
8 Echinops ritro
9 Salvia officinalis Purpurascens Group
10 Hippophae rhamnoides
11 Libertia formosa
12 Osteospermum jucundum
13 Escallonia 'Donard Radiance'
14 Artemisia stelleriana
15 Tamarix ramosissima
16 Rosa 'Fru Dagmar Hastrup'
17 Eryngium x oliverianum
18 Erigeron glaucus
19 Olearia macrodonta
20 Phormium tenax Purpureum Group
21 Hebe 'Rosie'
22 Lycium barbarum
23 Lavandula x intermedia 'Grappenhall'
24 Armeria maritima 'Alba'

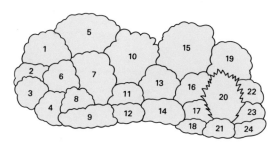

ALTERNATIVE PLANTING

With so many different kinds available, it would
be easy to fill a garden with hebes, and coastal
gardens are the perfect opportunity to make the
most of these evergreen shrubs. This scheme
replaces some of the plants with more hebes, with
contrasting foliage and masses of bright flowers.

HEBE SCHEME

2 *Hebe* x *franciscana* 'Variegata'

4 *Hebe* 'Caledonia'

7 *Hebe* 'Great Orme'

12 *Hebe* 'Red Edge'

13 *Hebe* 'La Séduisante'

23 *Hebe armstrongii*

WILDFLOWER GARDENS

IN GARDENS GRASS IS NO LONGER CONFINED TO THE GREEN SQUARE IN THE CENTRE OF THE PLOT; ITS ROLE HAS EXPANDED IN RECENT YEARS AS THE RANGE AND AVAILABILITY OF GRASSES HAS INCREASED. ORNAMENTAL GRASSES CAN BE PLANTED AS PART OF A TRADITIONAL BORDER SCHEME, OR NATIVE GRASSES CAN BE USED TO FORM THE BASIS OF A WILDFLOWER MEADOW. WILDFLOWER AREAS, ESPECIALLY IF THEY INCLUDE WATER IN THE FORM OF A POOL OR STREAM, ARE NOT ONLY ATTRACTIVE AND EASY TO MAINTAIN, BUT ALSO ACT AS WILDLIFE REFUGES, A VALUABLE RESOURCE IN URBAN AREAS. AND EVEN IN GARDENS WHERE THERE IS ONLY SPACE FOR ONE OR TWO TREES, YOU CAN TAKE ADVANTAGE OF THE CONDITIONS THEY PRODUCE TO PLANT A SHADY WOODLAND PLANTING FOR SPRING.

Corn marigolds and blue cornflowers are early invaders of the meadow, bringing summer colour until perennials become established.

BUTTERFLY BORDER

MANY GARDEN BUTTERFLIES ARE MOST ABUNDANT in late summer, when most plants are looking tired and have few flowers, so a butterfly border brings colour and life when other gardens are dull. This mixture of wildflowers, will self-seed, and late-flowering garden plants will attract clouds of insects. If the stems are left in winter the seedheads will attract finches to the garden. This planting suits most well-drained soils.

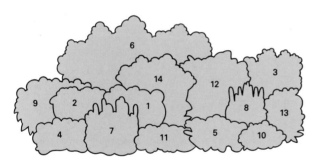

ALTERNATIVE PLANTING

Although annuals are often criticized for having no attraction to insects such as butterflies, many are useful, but avoid double-flowered cultivars. Butter-flies prefer purple flowers, so make these the basis of an annual scheme. You could add annuals to the main scheme in the early years to add mass.

ANNUAL SCHEME

- 3 *Callistephus chinensis* cultivars (single)
- 5 *Verbena* 'Blue Lagoon'
- 8 *Limonium sinuatum* 'Purple Monarch'
- 10 *Heliophila longifolia*
- 12 *Heliotropium* 'Chatsworth'
- 13 *Cosmos bipinnatus*

PLANTING GUIDE

1. *Achillea millefolium*
2. *Asclepias tuberosa*
3. *Aster novae-angliae*
4. *Coreopsis auriculata* 'Schnittgold'
5. *Daucus carota*
6. *Eupatorium purpureum* subsp. *maculatum*
7. *Liatris spicata*
8. *Lobelia cardinalis*
9. *Monarda didyma*
10. *Origanum vulgare*
11. *Sedum spectabile*
12. *Solidago odora*
13. *Succisa pratensis*
14. *Verbena bonariensis*

SCHEME FOR CHALK DOWNLAND

THE SOIL OF CHALK DOWNLAND is dry and poor in nutrients, which leads to fine-leaved, short grasses and an abundance of flowers. This scheme will thrive on any soil with a high pH and in full sun. As with any other planting in turf, the grass should be cut after the plants have set seed, and raked off to prevent the soil being enriched with nutrients, which would favour the grass. This scheme will provide colour in summer.

LATE-SPRING MEADOW

A WAY TO ATTRACT INSECTS to the garden is to convert a lawn into a wildflower meadow. If you have existing turf, simply adapt small plants and arrange these in groups in the lawn. Alternatively, clear some ground of weeds and sow a wildflower mixture with grasses. You will need to plant a few bulbs for extra colour. Cut the grass once the flowers have seeded, and again in late autumn. This planing suits moist, well-drained soil.

PLANTING GUIDE

1 *Cardamine pratensis*

2 *Bellis perennis*

3 *Fritillaria meleagris*

4 *Hyacinthoides non-scripta*

5 *Lamium galeobdolon*

6 *Lamium album*

7 *Lychnis flos-cuculi*

8 *Primula veris*

9 *Ranunculus acris*

10 *Silene dioica*

11 *Stellaria holostea* and *S. graminea*

12 *Taraxacum officinale*

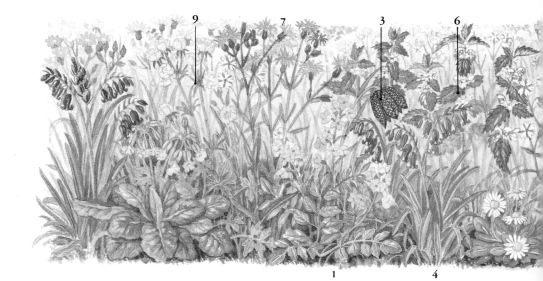

PLANTING GUIDE

1. *Campanula glomerata*
2. *Campanula rotundifolia*
3. *Centaurea nigra*
4. *Dianthus gratianopolitanus*

5. *Helianthemum nummularium*
6. *Linaria vulgaris*
7. *Linum perenne*
8. *Origanum vulgare*

9. *Reseda lutea*
10. *Salvia pratensis*
11. *Sanguisorba minor*
12. *Thymus polytrichus*

MIDSUMMER MEADOW

YOU WILL RECOGNIZE some popular garden plants among this colourful selection for a midsummer meadow. This scheme looks best on a fairly large scale because the plants are individually quite large and a hazy mixture is the aim. Try them in any average soil in full sun. After a few years some plants will begin to dominate because they are better adapted to your soil or your maintenance schedule. The timing of the summer cut is important: it should be as late as possible so that the seeds of later-flowering plants are not removed. Cut grass must be raked off or it will choke the more delicate plants. In the first year, annuals like corn marigolds and poppies can be sown, but these will be crowded out as the meadow develops.

1   2   3   4   5   6   7   8

PLANTING GUIDE

1. *Stokesia laevis*
2. *Filipendula vulgaris*
3. *Heliopsis helianthoides*
4. *Malva moschata*
5. *Ranunculus acris*
6. *Geranium pratense*

7. *Centaurea scabiosa*
8. *Galium verum*
9. *Trifolium pratense*
10. *Hypericum perforatum*
11. *Knautia arvensis*
12. *Polemonium caeruleum*

13. *Coreopsis lanceolata*
14. *Scabiosa columbaria*
15. *Rhinanthus major*
16. *Vicia cracca*

WETLAND WILDFLOWERS

PONDS ARE A MAGNET FOR WILDLIFE and open up a new world of planting opportunities. Some plants, like *Iris pseudacorus*, will grow in a pond, with their crowns covered with a little water, or in the moist soil at the margins, but most plants demand one or other situation. This scheme, shown in midsummer, includes plants for both moist and wet conditions and will give flowers and interest for a long period in summer.

PLANTING GUIDE

MARSHY MEADOW AREA

1 *Polygonum bistorta*

2 *Hibiscus moscheutos*

3 *Mentha aquatica*

4 *Lythrum salicaria*

5 *Iris versicolor*

6 *Filipendula ulmaria*

7 *Lobelia cardinalis*

8 *Eupatorium cannabinum*

9 *Stachys palustris*

10 *Trollius europaeus*

11 *Osmunda regalis*

POND SIDE

12 *Saururus cernuus*

13 *Menyanthes trifoliata*

14 *Iris pseudacorus*

15 *Butomus umbellatus*

16 *Ranunculus lingua*

WOODLAND PLANTING FOR LATE SPRING

THE LIGHT SHADE OF WOODLAND gives shelter to some of the most beautiful spring flowers. However, dry soil in dense shade is less suitable for the plants in this scene. Dig garden compost or leafmould into the soil, mulch around the plants and keep them well watered at first. Some will spread quickly while others will form small clumps.

1   2   3   4   5   6   7   8   9   10   11

PLANTING GUIDE

1. *Aquilegia canadensis*
2. *Galium odoratum*
3. *Primula elatior*
4. *Phlox stolonifera*
5. *Phegopteris hexagonoptera*
6. *Erythronium revolutum*
7. *Trillium grandiflorum*
8. *Polystichum acrostichoides*
9. *Sanguinaria canadensis*
10. *Helleborus foetidus*
11. *Viola riviniana*
12. *Convallaria majalis*
13. *Primula vulgaris*
14. *Dryopteris filix-mas*
15. *Dicentra eximia*
16. *Anemone nemorosa*
17. *Chrysogonum virginianum*
18. *Silene virginica*
19. *Mertensia pulmonarioides*

WOODLAND ON ACID SOIL

A WOODLAND GARDEN DOES NOT REQUIRE ACRES of land and the canopy of a single tree can provide shade without the mass of searching roots that often dry out the soil beneath a larger group of trees. An exotic woodland, shown here in late spring, relies on introduced plants rather than natives, although these may establish themselves in time. The main tree will suggest a colour scheme – a pink-flowered cherry looks good underplanted with deep green foliage, while the lime-green young foliage of this scarlet oak contrasts with orange, red and yellow leaves and flowers.

PLANTING GUIDE

1   *Rhododendron* Fabia Group

2   *Dryopteris affinis*

3   *Pieris japonica* 'Firecrest'

4   *Gymnocarpium dryopteris*

5   *Gaultheria procumbens*

6   *Quercus coccinea*

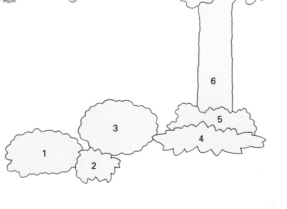

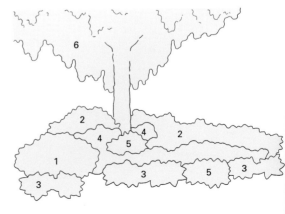

WOODLAND ON LIMY SOIL

CHERRIES THRIVE ON CHALK and this scheme is based around
the double, white cherry that provides the shade. In early spring
the ground is covered with flowers that reflect the freshness of
the cherry foliage and flowers. These include white hellebores
and snowdrops, pale yellow primroses and the pale green flowers
of the evergreen ribes. This arrangement can look sombre later
in summer but the addition of white dicentras and martagon
lilies, solomon's seal and variegated hostas will give interest.
Another, unusual plant is *Actaea alba*, which is colourful in late
summer, with pure white (but poisonous) berries.

PLANTING GUIDE

1. *Ribes laurifolium*
2. *Helleborus orientalis*
3. *Primula vulgaris*
4. *Galanthus nivalis*
5. *Polypodium vulgare* 'Cornubiense'
6. *Prunus avium* 'Plena'

WATER GARDENS

BRINGING WATER INTO THE GARDEN OPENS UP GREAT POSSIBILITIES FOR COMBINING PLANTS. FROM THE HUGE LEAVES OF GUNNERA TO SPIKY RUSHES AND ELEGANT PRIMULAS, THE OPTIONS FOR CONTRAST AND HARMONY ARE NUMEROUS. WATER ITSELF HAS MANY MOODS, AND THE PLANTING CAN BE DESIGNED TO REFLECT THIS. A QUIET AND CALMING POND, WITH STILL REFLECTIONS, WILL BE COMPLEMENTED BY COOL GREEN FOLIAGE. A POOL WITH A FOUNTAIN, FULL OF LIFE AND MOVEMENT, CALLS FOR BRIGHT PLUMES OF ASTILBES AND COLOURED FOLIAGE.

SOME POND PLANTS HAVE A REPUTATION FOR BEING INVASIVE BUT MOST CAN BE CONTROLLED BY GROWING THEM IN BASKETS. OTHERS ARE TENDER AND WILL NOT SURVIVE THE WINTER IN COLDER AREAS, BUT THEY ALL HAVE THEIR PART TO PLAY IN ONE OF THE MOST REWARDING FORMS OF GARDENING.

The majestic fronds of the royal fern (Osmunda) add an air of serenity to a pond in sun or shade.

FORMAL POOL

IN A SMALL GARDEN a formal pond often looks better than an informal one, and even if not planted with native species it will attract a wonderful range of wildlife. This scheme, shown here in midsummer, includes plants with a range of habits and they can all be planted in baskets on shelves in the pond. This is an easier way to control their growth than by making beds in the pond, where vigorous species can swamp more delicate ones. Submerged plants help keep the water clear, and water lilies, which cover the surface of the water, will help control blanketweed. However, part of the beauty of a pond is the sight of the water and its reflections, so leave gaps around the edge and keep some of the water surface clear of vegetation.

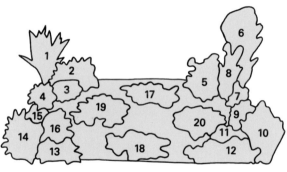

ALTERNATIVE PLANTING

In a very small area some water plants can be too vigorous and rapidly take over a pond. With a little searching you should be able to find dwarf forms of some water plants, especially water lilies, that will also grow in shallow water. As a general rule, variegated forms are slower-growing than the plain green forms, as well as more attractive for a long period.

SMALLER SCHEME

1 *Caltha palustris*
2 *Zantedeschia aethiopica* 'Little Gem'
3 *Acorus gramineus* 'Ogon'
4 *Eriophorum angustifolium*
5 *Juncus effusus* 'Spiralis'
6 *Nymphaea tetragona*
7 *Nymphaea* 'Pygmaea Helvola'
8 *Nymphaea* 'Pygmaea Rubra'

PLANTING GUIDE

1. *Iris pseudacorus* 'Variegata'
2. *Peltandra sagittifolia*
3. *Caltha palustris* 'Flore Pleno'
4. *Cotula coronopifolia*
5. *Zantedeschia aethiopica*
6. *Schoenoplectus lacustris*
7. *Veronica beccabunga*

8. *Iris laevigata*
9. *Sagittaria sagittifolia* 'Flore Pleno'
10. *Iris laevigata* 'Variegata'
11. *Myosotis scorpioides*
12. *Mentha aquatica*
13. *Houttuynia cordata* 'Flore Pleno'
14. *Pontederia cordata*

15. *Myriophyllum aquaticum*
16. *Saururus cernuus*
17. *Nymphaea* 'Amabilis'
18. *Nymphaea* 'Firecrest'
19. *Nymphaea* 'Escarboucle'
20. *Aponogeton distachyos*

INFORMAL POOL

WATER PLANTS OFTEN LOOK THEIR BEST in spring, but this planting
holds its interest throughout summer and even has colour and
interest in autumn with the white, bottlebrush flowers of cimicifuga
and the bronzing of the darmera leaves as they die. There is
a great variety of foliage shape and colour, and variegated
forms of filipendula and scrophularia provide colour. If
the pond has a waterproof liner, some of the
marginal plants may need extra watering
because they require moist conditions
and the soil surrounding the
pond may be dry.

PLANTING GUIDE

1. *Lobelia* 'Queen Victoria'
2. *Scrophularia auriculata* 'Variegata'
3. *Pontederia cordata*
4. *Myosotis scorpioides*
5. *Primula beesiana*
6. *Persicaria bistorta*
7. *Butomus umbellatus*
8. *Astilbe* 'Fanal'

9. *Rheum palmatum* 'Atrosanguineum'
10. *Veronica beccabunga*
11. *Cimicifuga simplex* Atropurpurea Group
12. *Caltha palustris* var. *palustris*
13. *Filipendula ulmaria* 'Aurea'
14. *Carex elata* 'Aurea'
15. *Iris sibirica*
16. *Primula denticulata*

17. *Darmera peltata*
18. *Menyanthes trifoliata*
19. *Lysichiton americanus*
20. *Peltandra sagittifolia*
21. *Nymphaea* 'Hermine'
22. *Nymphaea* 'Froebelii'
23. *Orontium aquaticum*

ALTERNATIVE PLANTING

If you are in a warm region, it is possible to adapt this scheme to include beautiful tender plants and tropical water lilies in shades not found in hardy plants. The addition of some larger leaves and new colours will bring a magical touch to the garden. In cool areas some of these plants can be put into the pond as temporary display plants in summer, but they will require protection from frost in winter.

WARM-CLIMATE SCHEME

- (5) *Acorus gramineus* 'Variegatus'
- (6) *Cyperus papyrus* 'Nanus'
- (8) *Thalia dealbata*
- (13) *Colocasia esculenta*
- (16) *Zantedeschia aethiopica* 'Green Goddess'
- (20) *Nymphaea* x *daubenyana*
- (21) *Nymphaea* 'Blue Beauty'
- (22) *Nymphaea* 'General Pershing'

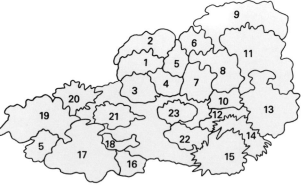

MINIMALIST SCHEME FOR FORMAL POOL

THIS FORMAL POOL, which has two levels of water and a linking waterfall, is suitable for a patio or formal terrace and brings the reflective quality of water near the home. The planting, shown here in early summer, is minimal to emphasize the water surface. Two floating plants are included; the azolla will rapidly spread in sunny, warm weather to form a mat of green that turns to crimson in winter. It can be invasive, but is easily raked off a small pool like this. The water hyacinth (*Eichhornia*) needs protection in winter. In warm climates it may also spread vigorously. The iris and schoenoplectus provide a vertical accent and their foliage is striped.

PLANTING GUIDE

1. *Azolla mexicana*
2. *Iris pseudacorus* 'Variegata'
3. *Schoenoplectus lacustris* 'Zebrinus'
4. *Nymphaea* 'Pink Sensation'
5. *Eichhornia crassipes*

WATER GARDEN IN A TUB

EVEN IF YOU DO NOT HAVE A GARDEN you can enjoy water gardening by planting in a half-barrel or large tub, shown here in late summer. Stand it in a semi-shaded position, especially if you wish to add a few fish, because the temperature of water in a tub in full sun can rise quickly. Choose plants carefully and use the dwarf water lily and azolla to cover the water surface to prevent the growth of algae and blanketweed. Fortunately, it is easy to pull out surplus weed.

PLANTING GUIDE

1 *Myriophyllum aquaticum*

2 *Typha minima*

3 *Juncus effusus* 'Spiralis'

4 *Iris laevigata*

5 *Azolla mexicana*

6 *Nymphaea* 'Pygmaea Helvola'

WILDLIFE POOL AND BOG

A WILDLIFE POND does not have to be filled with native plants, but these often have special benefits for insects. A wildlife pond is also better if planned and planted informally with a mixture of plants so that, if any are food sources for insects, leaf damage does not spoil the display. If grass or pebbles can create a gently sloping beach to provide easy access for amphibians and hedgehogs, the pond will be a resource and not a hazard. This scheme, shown in late spring, uses plants with small flowers that attract insects, and dense leaf cover to protect frogs and toads during the day. The plants selected will flower throughout summer and into autumn.

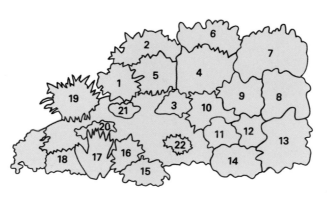

ALTERNATIVE PLANTING

In a small garden every plant has to work extra hard at providing some colour and interest. Although flowers may be the pinnacle of a plant's beauty, leaves last much longer and should never be simply dismissed as just green. Pond plants have a variety of leaf shapes and sizes and these alternatives add to this diversity with the attraction of variegation.

VARIEGATED SCHEME

20 *Carex elata* 'Aurea'
21 *Iris laevigata* 'Variegata'
11 *Mentha* x *gracilis* 'Variegata'
6   *Scrophularia auriculata* 'Variegata'
9   *Typha latifolia* 'Variegata'
16 *Ajuga reptans* 'Catlin's Giant'
13 *Filipendula ulmaria* 'Aurea'
3   *Lysimachia nummularia* 'Aurea'

PLANTING GUIDE

1. *Calla palustris*
2. *Persicaria bistorta*
3. *Veronica beccabunga*
4. *Iris pseudacorus*
5. *Butomus umbellatus*
6. *Senecio smithii*
7. *Lythrum salicaria*
8. *Filipendula ulmaria*

9. *Glyceria maxima* var. *variegata*
10. *Sagittaria sagittifolia*
11. *Ranunculus flammula*
12. *Mentha aquatica*
13. *Aruncus dioicus*
14. *Cardamine pratensis*
15. *Caltha palustris*
16. *Alisma plantago-aquatica*

17. *Acorus calamus* 'Variegatus'
18. *Eriophorum angustifolium*
19. *Carex pendula*
20. *Nymphoides peltata*
21. *Azolla mexicana*
22. *Stratiotes aloides*

ROCK GARDEN POOL

INFORMAL POOLS SIT HAPPILY amid rock gardens and the change of levels provides an ideal opportunity to incorporate a waterfall or streams. The sloping soil level among the rocks gives a graduation of moisture with the result that a range of plants can be accommodated in optimum growing conditions within a fairly restricted area. In some places, the soil around the pool may be so dry that ordinary alpines can be planted, growing close to moisture-lovers in damper areas. Cascading plants like *Saxifraga* 'Tumbling Waters' can be positioned to tumble over the rocks, while small soil pockets at the margins of the pond can be planted with bog plants that are not true aquatics. This planting is shown in early to midsummer.

PLANTING GUIDE

1   *Alchemilla mollis*

2   *Anthyllis montana*

3   *Aquilega alpina*

4   *Astilbe chinensis* var. *pumila*

5   *Caltha palustris*

6   *Dactylorhiza elata*

7   *Genista lydia*

8   *Gunnera magellanica*

9   *Hosta sieboldiana*

10   *Hosta* 'Frances Williams'

11   *Iris sanguinea*

12   *Primula prolifera*

13   *Primula pulverulenta*

14   *Primula rosea*

15   *Saxifraga* 'Tumbling Waters'

16   *Trollius* x *cultorum* 'Canary Bird'

17   *Trollius pumilus*

STRUCTURES AND FEATURES

MOST GARDENS CONTAIN MORE THAN PLANTS ALONE AND HAVE FEATURES WHOSE FUNCTION IS EITHER FUNCTIONAL OR DECORATIVE. THESE STRUCTURES ARE USUALLY INSTANT, PROVIDING HEIGHT OR INTEREST IMMEDIATELY, BUT THEY ALSO CHANGE WITH THE PASSAGE OF TIME, BECOMING WEATHERED WITH AGE OR COVERED WITH CLIMBERS OR CREEPERS AS THEY BECOME ASSIMILATED INTO THE GARDEN. PLANTING PLAYS A VITAL PART IN THIS PROCESS – POSITIONING LOW-GROWING PLANTS SO THAT THEY CREEP OVER THE EDGES OF PATHS PROVIDES AN INSTANT LINK BETWEEN THE HARD AND SOFT SURFACES OF THE GARDEN. IT IS EASY TO DEVELOP A THEME BETWEEN FEATURES AND PLANTS; ROUGH-HEWN TIMBER IN WOODLAND GARDENS, JAPANESE PLANTS SURROUNDING JAPANESE ORNAMENTS OR GRASSES AND SEDGES AROUND MODERN SCULPTURE ARE JUST A FEW OF THE MANY OPTIONS.

An arch provides support for a rose, but is also a focal point, giving interest to the border and tempting us to explore the background.

SHADED TERRACE IN LATE WINTER

EVERGREEN FOLIAGE PLAYS A LARGE PART in this scheme for shade. The clipped shrubs make link between the formality of the drive and the informal planting in the rest of the garden, and look good in winter. The leathery leaves of bergenia provide extra winter interest, turning shades of red and purple.

PLANTING GUIDE

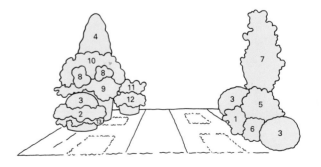

1. *Bergenia cordifolia*
2. *Brassica oleracea*
3. *Buxus sempervirens* 'Suffruticosa'
4. *Buxus sempervirens* 'Elegantissima'
5. *Daphne odora* 'Aureomarginata'
6. *Euonymus fortunei* 'Emerald Gaiety'
7. *Garrya elliptica*
8. *Hebe buxifolia*
9. *Hedera helix*
10. *Helleborus foetidus*
11. *Narcissus* 'Tête-à-tête'
12. *Valeriana phu* 'Aurea'
13. *Vinca minor* 'Variegata'

SUNNY AREA IN MIDSUMMER

IT USUALLY TAKES SEVERAL YEARS for shrubs to reach their full height so for the impatient gardener the biennial onopordums that frame this pair of summer borders are useful plants. They achieve their dramatic climax after only two seasons. Grow new plants from seed each year as replacements.

PLANTING GUIDE

1. *Acaena saccaticupula* 'Blue Haze'
2. *Artemisia* 'Powis Castle'
3. *Cistus* 'Silver Pink'
4. *Erigeron karvinskianus*
5. *Eryngium giganteum*
6. *Euphorbia characias* subsp. *wulfenii*
7. *Hebe* 'Red Edge'
8. *Lavandula stoechas* subsp. *pedunculata*
9. *Linaria purpurea* 'Canon Went'
10. *Onopordum acanthium*
11. *Romneya coulteri*
12. *Salvia sclarea* var. *turkestanica*
13. *Thymus serpyllum*
14. *Verbascum olympicum*

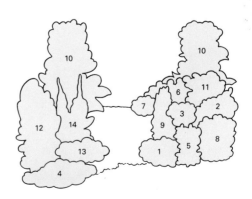

OUTDOOR ROOM

OUTDOOR SITTING AND DINING AREAS are usually sheltered and sunny, and the protection provided by walls, fences and trellis suits many plants that might be buffeted and damaged in more open positions. The disadvantage is that such planting areas are also likely to be sheltered from the rain, so the soil tends to be dry. This scheme, which is suitable for a well-drained site, is shown in late summer.

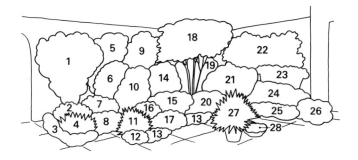

PLANTING GUIDE

1. *Aloysia triphylla*
2. *Rosmarinus officinalis* 'Benenden Blue'
3. *Stachys byzantina* 'Silver Carpet'
4. *Sisyrinchium striatum* 'Aunt May'
5. *Robinia hispida*
6. *Myrtus communis*
7. *Coronilla valentina*
8. *Epilobium canum*
9. *Vitis vinifera* 'Purpurea'
10. *Olearia stellulata*

11. *Yucca filamentosa* 'Bright Edge'
12. *Thymus* 'Doone Valley'
13. *Helianthemum* 'Rhodanthe Carneum'
14. *Abelia* x *grandiflora*
15. *Nerine bowdenii*
16. *Punica granatum* var. *nana*
17. *Ceratostigma willmottianum*
18. *Aralia elata*
19. *Pittosporum* 'Garnettii'
20. *Santolina pinnata*

21. *Euphorbia characias* subsp. *wulfenii*
22. *Ceanothus* 'Burkwoodii'
23. *Amaryllis belladonna*
24. *Ruta graveolens* 'Jackman's Blue'
25. *Origanum laevigatum*
26. *Convolvulus cneorum*
27. *Cordyline australis* 'Torbay Dazzler'
28. *Echeveria secunda*

ALTERNATIVE PLANTING

In the shelter of a garden room many tender plants
can be used in containers to add extra colour and
contrasts of form. A group of pots can be moved
where needed to cover gaps in the border, and
lilies can be brought from another area of the
garden to bring colour and scent. Most will require
protection from frost, but in mild climates can be
left in the garden all winter.

CONTAINER PLANTS

1. *Lilium* 'Casa Blanca'
2. *Cyathea australis*
3. *Trachycarpus fortunei*
4. *Acca sellowiana*
5. *Sempervivum* 'Commander Hay'
6. *Canna* 'Roi Humbert'
7. *Plumbago auriculata*
8. *Brugmansia* x *candida* 'Grand Marnier'

SHADY HOUSE WALL IN EARLY SUMMER

SHADY WALLS present a challenge for gardeners, but many plants will thrive in cool shade. This planting makes a restful scene with pale flowers and different greens and variegated leaves. The ivy and climbing hydrangea are self-clinging and no trellis is required.

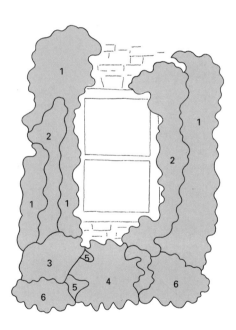

PLANTING GUIDE

1. *Hydrangea anomala* subsp. *petiolaris*
2. *Hedera hibernica*
3. *Polygonatum* x *hybridum*
4. *Polystichum setiferum*
5. *Meconopsis cambrica*
6. *Hosta* 'Francee'

COTTAGE PLANTING FOR A DRY-STONE WALL

THE INFORMAL APPEARANCE of a dry-stone wall lends itself to a cottage-garden planting. This scheme combines old favourites like rambling roses and foxgloves with more exotic plants such as the evergreen hebe and passionflowers that will appreciate the reflected heat from the wall.

PLANTING GUIDE

1. *Rosa* 'Dorothy Perkins'
2. *Lathyrus grandiflorus*
3. *Passiflora caerulea*
4. *Hebe* 'Red Edge'
5. *Ruta graveolens* 'Jackman's Blue'
6. *Digitalis purpurea*
7. *Caryopteris* x *clandonensis*

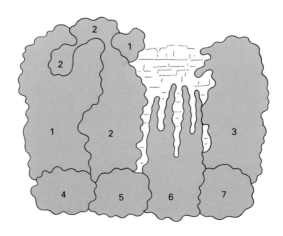

SUNNY WALL

A SUNNY WALL PROVIDES the opportunity
to grow tender plants that may not thrive
in the open garden. This scheme, shown
in late summer, includes plants with deep
green and silver leaves, and the repetition
of gypsophila and several lavenders helps
to prevent a bitty effect in a border that
is packed with contrasts. Most of the
plants in this scheme are evergreens, so
there is interest throughout the year.

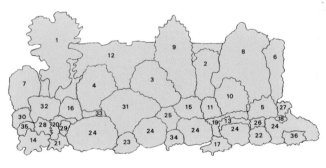

PLANTING GUIDE

ON THE WALL

1. *Azara microphylla* 'Variegata'
2. *Buddleja crispa*
3. *Bupleurum fruticosum*
4. *Carpenteria californica*
5. *Ceratostigma willmottianum*
6. *Clematis* 'Etoile Rose'
7. *Daphne bholua*
8. *Itea ilicifolia*
9. *Pittosporum tenuifolium* 'Silver Queen'
10. *Rosa* x *odorata* 'Mutabilis'
11. *Senecio viravira*
12. *Solanum jasminoides* 'Album'

FLOWER BED AT BASE OF WALL

13. *Arum creticum*
14. *Bergenia ciliata*
15. *Cistus* 'Silver Pink'
16. *Convolvulus cneorum*
17. *Convolvulus sabatius*
18. *Cyclamen coum*
19. *Zauschneria californica* 'Dublin'

20 *Erodium pelargoniiflorum*

21 *Euphorbia myrsinites*

22 *Geranium renardii*

23 *Geranium traversii* var. *elegans*

24 *Gypsophila* 'Rosenschleier'

25 x *Halimiocistus wintonensis* 'Merrist
    Wood Cream'

26 *Helianthemum* 'Beech Park Red'

27 *Helleborus* x *sternii* 'Boughton Beauty'

28 *Iris* 'Cherry Garden'

29 *Iris* 'Green Spot'

30 *Iris unguicularis*

31 *Lavandula* x *intermedia* 'Hidcote Giant'

32 *Lavandula lanata*

33 *Nerine undulata*

34 *Origanum* 'Kent Beauty'

35 *Origanum rotundifolium*

36 *Yucca filamentosa* 'Variegata'

CREVICE PLANTING IN SUN

THE PERFECT DRAINAGE provided by a dry-stone wall is ideal for many alpine plants that dislike moisture around their crowns, especially in winter. It is better to insert plants as the wall is built, but small plants can be inserted later if they are watered regularly until established. Many plants, such as the campanula, will run through the joints in the wall and others may self-seed. The scheme is shown in midsummer.

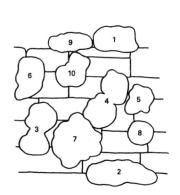

PLANTING GUIDE

1. *Acantholimon glumaceum*
2. *Campanula cochleariifolia*
3. *Asplenium ceterach*
4. *Erinus alpinus*
5. *Lewisia cotyledon*
6. *Penstemon newberryi*
7. *Saponaria ocymoides*
8. *Saxifraga longifolia*
9. *Sedum acre*
10. *Sempervivum montanum*

CREVICE PLANTING IN SHADE

THE COOL CONDITIONS of a shady wall, shown here in late spring, are ideal for many ferns and other plants that need perfect drainage but will not tolerate drought. If the wall retains soil, the range of plants that can be grown is increased. In dry weather watering may be needed to ensure that the iris and pratia survive, though cymbalaria and corydalis will run and self-seed quickly.

PLANTING GUIDE

1. *Arenaria balearica*
2. *Asplenium trichomanes*
3. *Corydalis lutea*
4. *Cymbalaria muralis*
5. *Haberlea rhodopensis*
6. *Iris cristata*
7. *Pratia pedunculata*
8. *Ramonda myconi*

SHADY WALL

IN THE SHADE CAST BY A WALL, there is protection from wind and relatively moist soil, unlike under a tree where the roots dry out the soil. This enables a much wider range of plants to flourish. Narrow borders by house walls should be avoided because the eaves can cause a 'rain shadow' stopping water reaching the soil, and in this scheme the border is at least 90cm (3ft) wide. Shown here in spring, the planting could be enhanced with spring-flowering bulbs such as purple crocus among the green flowers of hellebores, yellow daffodils through the euphorbia and white *Scilla sibirica* with the purple violas. Lilies could be added to give fragrance in summer. Many of these plants are evergreen and look good throughout the year – an important factor for any planting near the house, where it will be seen every day.

PLANTING GUIDE

1. *Chaenomeles* x *superba* 'Rowallane'
2. *Arum italicum* subsp. *italicum*
3. *Hedera helix* 'Glacier'
4. *Choisya ternata* Sundance
5. *Euphorbia amygdaloides* var. *robbiae*
6. *Cotoneaster lacteus*
7. *Digitalis grandiflora*
8. *Lonicera nitida* 'Baggesen's Gold'
9. *Bergenia* 'Sunningdale'
10. *Rhamnus alaternus* 'Argenteovariegata'
11. *Mahonia pinnata*
12. *Iris foetidissima* var. *citrina*
13. *Dryopteris filix-mas*
14. *Jasminum nudiflorum*
15. *Aucuba japonica* 'Rozannie'
16. *Helleborus argutifolius*
17. *Viola riviniana* Purpurea Group
18. *Garrya elliptica*
19. *Euonymus fortunei* 'Emerald Gaiety'
20. *Brunnera macrophylla*
21. *Geranium macrorrhizum*
22. *Rhododendron yakushimanum*

ALTERNATIVE PLANTING

The same basic layout can be used to create a pastel scheme in shades of pink instead of bright yellow and red. There are many small bulbs that would fit into this colour scheme and white and pink daffodils such as 'Mount Hood' and 'Salome' would be appropriate. Variegated ivies could be used more widely on the walls and there are different leaf shapes and colours to brighten all seasons.

PINK SCHEME

- **1** *Chaenomeles* x *superba* 'Pink Lady'
- **4** *Choisya ternata*
- **7** *Digitalis purpurea* 'Sutton's Apricot'
- **8** *Lonicera nitida* 'Silver Beauty'
- **11** *Photinia* x *fraseri* 'Red Robin'
- **12** *Iris foetidissima* 'Variegata'
- **14** *Abeliophyllum distichum*
- **16** *Helleborus orientalis*

COVERING FENCES

FENCES CAN BE COVERED WITH a combination
of climbers and self-supporting shrubs. The
latter provide a permanent framework over
which seasonal colour, in the form of scrambling
eccremocarpus, sweet peas (*Lathyrus*) or golden
hops (*Humulus*), can be introduced.

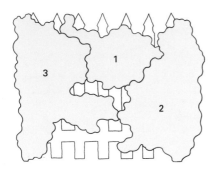

PLANTING GUIDE (midsummer)

1. *Vitis vinifera* 'Incana'
2. *Lonicera japonica* 'Halliana'
3. *Eccremocarpus scaber*

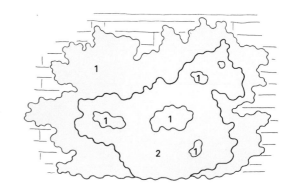

PLANTING GUIDE (early summer)

1. *Ceanothus impressus*
2. *Lathyrus rotundifolius*

PLANTING GUIDE (late summer)

1. *Humulus lupulus* 'Aureus'
2. *Actinidia deliciosa*
3. *Hedera canariensis* 'Gloire de Marengo'

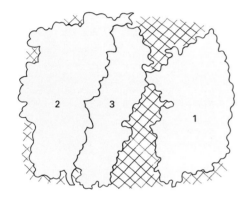

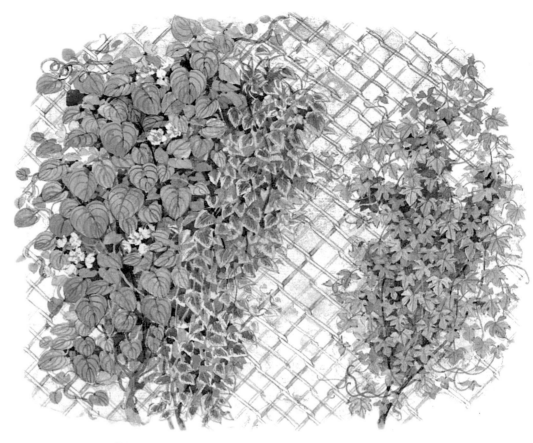

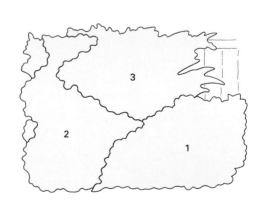

PLANTING GUIDE (midwinter)

1. *Choisya ternata*
2. *Hedera helix* 'Buttercup'
3. *Jasminum nudiflorum*

SUNNY STEPS IN LATE SUMMER

IN A FORMAL SETTING symmetrical planting beside steps gives a calm elegance. On this well-drained bank a collection of blue-flowered plants that combine silver foliage, fragrance and diverse habits look at their best in late summer. The height of the bank is emphasized by placing the tallest and most eye-catching plants at the top. The majestic yuccas and agapanthus draw the eye up the steps while trailing plants mask the edges.

PLANTING GUIDE

1 *Aconitum* 'Bressingham Spire'

2 *Agapanthus* Headbourne hybrids

3 *Buglossoides purpurocaerulea*

4 *Ceanothus* x *delileanus* 'Gloire de Versailles'

5 *Hebe* 'Pewter Dome'

6 *Lavandula angustifolia*

7 *Nepeta* 'Six Hills Giant'

8 *Perovskia* 'Blue Spire'

9 *Viola cornuta*

10 *Yucca gloriosa*

SHADY WOODLAND STEPS IN LATE SPRING

THESE RUSTIC STEPS made of split, round posts are edged with grass and a border of woodland plants that looks natural. Small, creeping plants such as soleirolia, ivy and lysimachia run along in front of the risers, enjoying the moist dappled shade. Their growth is controlled simply by using the steps.

PLANTING GUIDE

1. *Astrantia major* subsp. *involucrata* 'Shaggy'
2. *Cardamine trifolia*
3. *Cynoglossum nervosum*
4. *Dryopteris filix-mas*
5. *Gentiana asclepiadea*
6. *Hedera helix* 'Hazel'
7. *Iris foetidissima* 'Variegata'
8. *Lamium maculatum*
9. *Lysimachia nummularia*
10. *Polypodium vulgare*
11. *Silene fimbriata*
12. *Skimmia japonica* 'Rubella'
13. *Smyrnium perfoliatum*
14. *Soleirolia soleirolii*
15. *Uvularia grandiflora*

PLANTING BY PATHS

ONE OF THE ADVANTAGES of planting in borders next to paths is that the plants can be allowed to spill over the edge, and the flowers will not be splashed by soil. The plants are also easy to reach and see, so it is the perfect place for special gems that deserve careful observation. These schemes, shown in early summer, are for a shady brick path (below), a sunny path of granite setts (right above) and a stone path (right below).

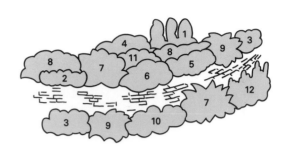

PLANTING GUIDE

1   *Cimicifuga racemosa*

2   *Convallaria majalis*

3   *Euphorbia amygdalioides* var. *robbiae*

4   *Euphorbia palustris*

5   *Geranium renardii*

6   *Hosta* 'Honeybells'

7   *Matteuccia struthiopteris*

8   *Polygonatum* x *hybridum*

9   *Polystichum setiferum*

10   *Pulmonaria angustifolia*

11   *Smilacina racemosa*

12   *Tiarella cordifolia*

PLANTING GUIDE

1. *Acanthus spinosus*
2. *Allium hollandicum*
3. *Artemisia arborescens*
4. *Lavandula angustifolia* 'Munstead'
5. *Melianthus major*
6. *Nepeta nervosa*
7. *Perovskia* 'Blue Spire'
8. *Rosa* 'Ballerina'
9. *Ruta graveolens* 'Jackman's Blue'
10. *Santolina chamaecyparissus*
11. *Sedum* 'Herbstfreude'
12. *Stachys byzantina* 'Cotton Boll'
13. *Viola cornuta*

PLANTING GUIDE

1. *Allium hollandicum* 'Purple Sensation'
2. *Atriplex hortensis* var. *rubra*
3. *Campanula latiloba* 'Hidcote Amethyst'
4. *Cistus* x *purpureus*
5. *Erysimum* 'Bowles' Mauve'
6. *Fuchsia magellanica* 'Versicolor'
7. *Hebe* 'Mrs Winder'
8. *Lavandula stoechas*
9. *Papaver orientale* 'Patty's Plum'
10. *Penstemon* 'Raven'
11. *Salvia officinalis* Purpurascens Group
12. *Sedum telephium* 'Atropurpureum'
13. *Viola riviniana* Purpurea Group
14. *Weigela florida* 'Foliis Purpureis'

PERGOLAS AND ARCHES

PERGOLAS AND ARCHES can be used to divide or connect areas of the garden, and provide the ideal place to grow climbing plants, especially those with hanging flowers, such as wisteria, which are displayed to perfection when viewed from below. Plant around the base of the supports, to mask the leafless stems of the climbers. The scheme below left is shown in late summer and the scheme below right in midsummer.

PLANTING GUIDE

1. *Wisteria floribunda*
2. *Clematis* 'Perle d'Azur'
3. *Rosa* 'Sanders' White Rambler'
4. *Solanum jasminoides* 'Album'
5. *Brunnera macrophylla*

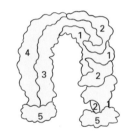

PLANTING GUIDE

1. *Clematis flammula*
2. *Clematis* 'Jackmanii Superba'
3. *Clematis rehderiana*
4. *Jasminum officinale* 'Argenteovariegatum'
5. *Lonicera periclymenum* 'Graham Thomas'
6. *Nepeta* 'Six Hills Giant'
7. *Rosa mulliganii*
8. *Solanum crispum* 'Glasnevin'
9. *Vitis vinifera* 'Purpurea'

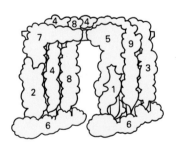

GARDEN SEAT IN MIDSUMMER

THE GARDEN SEAT IN THIS SCHEME fulfils two functions – it is not only the focal point of the vista, but also a place to sit and relax. The surrounding planting is made up of perfumed plants and foliage and flowers in pale and pastel colours to give an air of serenity and restfulness. A clump of fragrant thyme is planted in front of the bench; it releases its pungent aroma when crushed underfoot.

PLANTING GUIDE

1. *Buddleja alternifolia*
2. *Dictamnus albus* var. *purpureus*
3. *Foeniculum vulgare*
4. *Geranium macrorrhizum*
5. *Lathyrus odoratus*
6. *Lavandula angustifolia*
7. *Matthiola incana*
8. *Nepeta sibirica*
9. *Nicotiana sylvestris*
10. *Philadelphus coronarius*
11. *Rosa rubiginosa*
12. *Rosmarinus officinalis*
13. *Ruta graveolens* 'Jackman's Blue'
14. *Salvia officinalis*
15. *Thymus vulgaris*

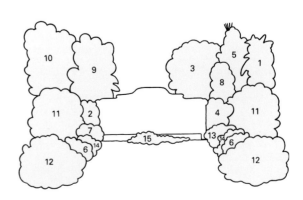

SUNNY BANK

LAWN GRASS DOES NOT GROW WELL on poor soil on a sunny bank, so instead of struggling with turf why not install some steps and turn the problem into a colourful feature with drought-tolerant plants that will look especially good in early summer as shown? Correct planting is important and it is easier to start at the top of the slope. Leave a slight depression around each plant so that water can be directed at their roots and will not run down the slope. If the slope is very steep it is best to make low terraces with wooden planks held in place with tree stakes cut to length and driven into the soil. A bark mulch will help to reduce evaporation of water from the soil when the plants are getting established. Plant spring-flowering bulbs for extra interest and colour.

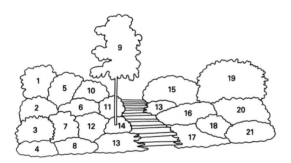

ALTERNATIVE PLANTING

If the site is sheltered and frost-free and you wish to create a less mounded and more exotic planting scheme, some of the more traditional plants can be substituted with spiky plants and grasses. Ornamental grasses give a long season of interest, and although their flowers are small they provide constant movement in the border. Yuccas and phormiums give a tropical touch.

MEDITERRANEAN SCHEME

1   *Phormium* 'Dazzler'

3   *Convolvulus cneorum*

9   *Genista aetnensis*

13 *Yucca filamentosa*

14 *Festuca glauca* 'Blaufuchs'

17 *Astelia chathamica*

18 *Corokia* x *virgata* 'Yellow Wonder'

20 *Stipa gigantea*

PLANTING GUIDE

1. *Rosa rugosa* 'Alba'
2. *Lupinus arboreus*
3. *Cotoneaster microphyllus*
4. x *Halimiocistus* 'Merrist Wood Cream'
5. *Hypericum* 'Hidcote'
6. *Ceanothus thyrsiflorus* var. *repens*
7. *Genista lydia*
8. *Juniperus communis* 'Repanda'

9. *Betula pendula* 'Laciniata'
10. *Phlomis fruticosa*
11. *Lonicera pileata*
12. *Prunus laurocerasus* 'Otto Luyken'
13. *Hedera helix* 'Green Ripple'
14. *Armeria maritima* 'Vindictive'
15. *Cistus* x *hybridus*
16. *Lavandula vera*

17. *Hedera helix* 'Manda's Crested'
18. *Centranthus ruber atrococcineus*
19. *Cytisus* 'Zeelandia'
20. *Rosa* x *jacksonii* 'Max Graf'
21. *Nepeta* 'Six Hills Giant'

SPECIALIST GARDENS

THERE ARE AS MANY TYPES OF GARDENER AS THERE ARE PLANTS. SOME USE PLANTS AS SHAPES, COLOURS AND TEXTURES TO CREATE WORKS OF ART, WHILE OTHERS LOVE THE PLANTS FOR THEMSELVES AND ARE COLLECTORS. THOSE WHO GROW EDIBLE PLANTS HAVE THE ADDED INCENTIVE OF GROWING CROPS FAR MORE SATISFYING THAN ANYTHING THAT CAN BE BOUGHT IN THE SHOPS. FOR PLANT COLLECTORS THE HEALTH AND SUCCESS OF THEIR PLANTS IS MORE IMPORTANT THAN THE WAY THE GARDEN LOOKS AND ALL SORTS OF STRANGE STRUCTURES MAY APPEAR TO PROTECT THEM FROM COLD, WET OR WIND. AREAS WITHIN THE GARDEN MAY BE MODIFIED TO PRODUCE THE PARTICULAR CONDITIONS NEEDED BY CERTAIN PLANTS. SPECIALIST GARDENS OFTEN HAVE A DIFFERENT CHARM TO OTHERS, AND AFTER THE FIRST CURSORY GLANCE, CLOSER OBSERVATION OFFERS MORE INTEREST AS THE INDIVIDUAL PLANTS ARE STUDIED.

Herb gardens are a popular type of specialist garden because of the wide range of productive plants that can be grown, and their historical interest.

GARDEN OF OLD ROSES

OLD-FASHIONED ROSES have beauty and wonderful scent, but most flower for a relatively short period in early midsummer. This garden includes other cottage-garden plants that cover the bare soil and flower with, and after, the roses, and all will thrive in rich, moist, but well-drained soil. Most old roses have blooms in shades of purple and pink, so the complementary plants reflect that colour range.

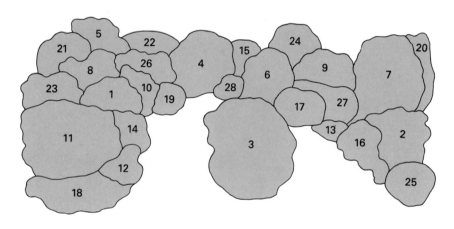

PLANTING GUIDE

ROSES

1. *R.* 'Camaïeux'
2. *R.* 'Cardinal de Richelieu'
3. *R.* 'Climbing Cécile Brünner'
4. *R.* 'Charles de Mills'
5. *R.* 'Fantin-Latour'
6. *R. gallica* 'Versicolor'
7. *R.* 'Great Maiden's Blush'
8. *R.* 'Marchesa Boccella'
9. *R.* 'Robert le Diable'
10. *R.* 'Tour de Malakoff'
11. *R.* 'William Lobb'

ACCOMPANYING PLANTS

12. *Astrantia major rosea*
13. *Astrantia major* 'Sunningdale Variegated'
14. *Campanula persicifolia* double blue
15. *Campanula pyramidalis*
16. *Geranium* x *oxonianum* 'Wargrave Pink'
17. *Geranium pratense* 'Plenum Caeruleum'
18. *Geranium procurrens*
19. *Tanacetum parthenium* 'Aureum'
20. *Alcea rosea*
21. *Lilium auratum*
22. *Lilium* Green Magic Group
23. *Lilium martagon* var. *album*
24. *Lilium regale*
25. *Nepeta racemosa*
26. *Salvia* x *superba*
27. *Sisyrinchium striatum*
28. *Stachys byzantina*

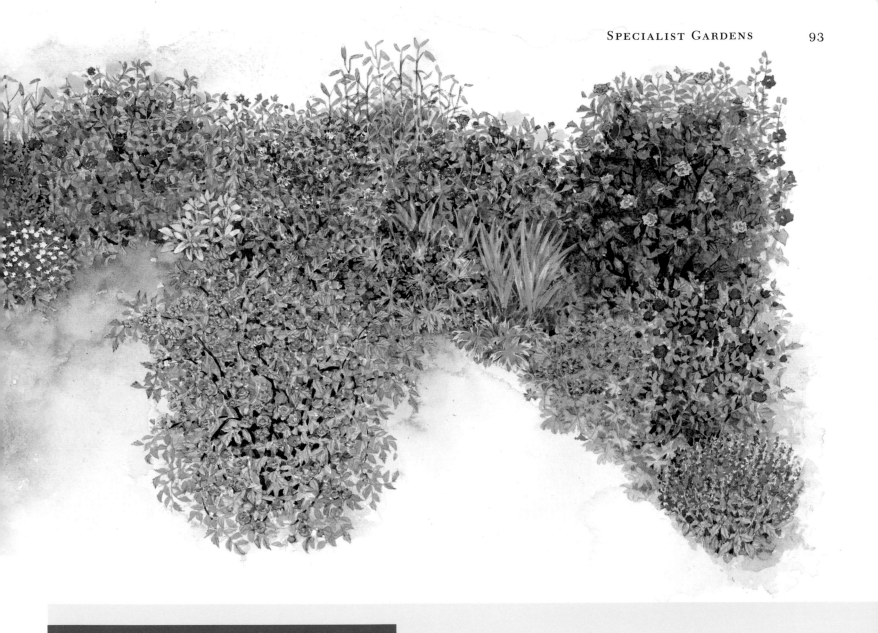

ALTERNATIVE PLANTING

The breeding work by rose-grower David Austin has brought the English Roses to our gardens. These combine the beauty and fragrance of old roses with the repeat-flowering qualities of modern roses. If these are substituted in this rose garden the flowering time will be extended. There is also a greater colour range so that a wider choice of underplanting is available.

ENGLISH ROSE SCHEME

1. R. Ambridge Rose
2. R. Charmain
3. R. Cressida
4. R. Gertrude Jekyll
5. R. Heritage
6. R. Mary Rose
7. R. Sharifa Asma
8. R. Lucetta

FORMAL HERB GARDEN

HERB GARDENS CAN LOOK bare in winter
because many perennial herbs die down to
ground level, and some of the most useful,
including chervil, summer savory and basil, are
annuals that must be replaced each spring.
To counter this, herbs are often grown
in a formal, well-structured
setting, with dwarf hedges and
straight paths, often around a
central feature such as a
sundial, bird bath or
clipped bay tree. Golden
and variegated herbs can
be planted to provide
extra colour.

PLANTING GUIDE

1. Apple mint (*Mentha suaveolens*)
2. Bay (*Laurus nobilis*)
3. Chives (*Allium schoenoprasum*)
4. Cotton lavender (*Santolina chamaecyparissus*)
5. Curry plant (*Helichrysum italicum*)
6. Double roman chamomile (*Chamaemelum nobile* 'Flore Pleno')
7. Dwarf box (*Buxus sempervirens* 'Suffruticosa')
8. French lavender (*Lavandula stoechas*)
9. Golden balm (*Melissa officinalis* 'Aurea')
10. Golden sage (*Salvia officinalis* 'Icterina')
11. Marjoram (*Origanum majorana*)
12. Nasturtium (*Tropaeolum majus*)
13. Parsley (*Petroselinum crispum*)
14. Purple basil (*Ocimum basilicum* 'Dark Opal')
15. Purple sage (*Salvia officinalis* Purpurascens Group)
16. Rosemary (*Rosmarinus officinalis*)
17. Summer savory (*Satureja hortensis*)
18. Thyme (*Thymus* species)
19. Tricolour sage (*Salvia officinalis* 'Tricolor')

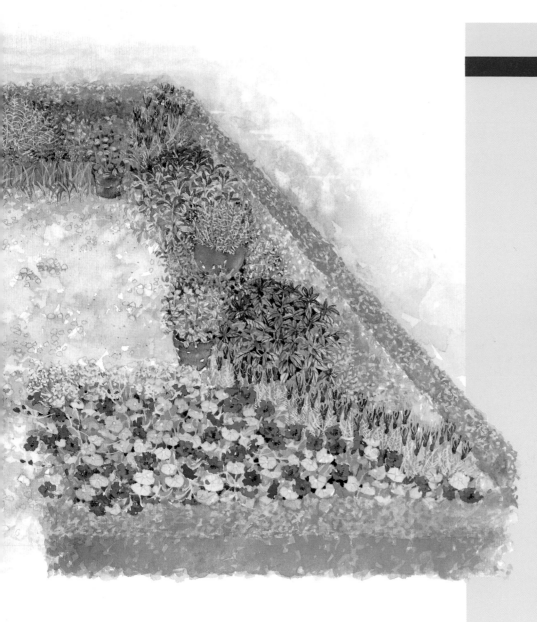

ALTERNATIVE PLANTING

A strong framework is essential for a herb garden to look good all year, but there are other plants that can be used to form the low hedges, apart from the traditional box. The advantage of box is that it is neat and evergreen and only requires cutting once a year, but other dwarf shrubs will make an interesting contrast, and could be used to edge beds within the main framework.

EDGING PLANTS

Rosa Little Bo-peep

Santolina rosmarinifolia

Santolina pinnata 'Edward Bowles'

Teucrium chamaedrys 'Nanum'

Lavandula angustifolia 'Dwarf Blue'

Iberis sempervirens

Euonymus fortunei 'Minimus'

Ilex crenata

AN ORNAMENTAL KITCHEN GARDEN

THE POTAGER or ornamental kitchen garden, shown here in late summer, demonstrates that many edible plants have great beauty, especially those cultivars with coloured foliage. For healthy vegetables, it is sensible to practise crop rotation to ensure strong growth and prevent the build-up of soil pests and diseases.

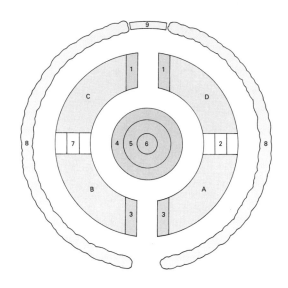

PLANTING GUIDE

1 Asparagus

2 Cucumber

3 Jerusalem artichoke

4 Lettuce 'Lollo Rosso'

5 Peas

6 Red orache

7 Runner beans

8 Blackberries, loganberries, blackcurrants

9 Vine *Vitis vinifera* 'Purpurea'

ROTATION CROPS

A Tubers and root crops	B Brassicas and leeks	C Peas and beans	D Salad and other crops
Beetroot	Brussels sprouts	Dwarf broad beans	Endive
Carrots	Cabbages	Dwarf French beans	Garlic
Parsnips	Cauliflowers	Dwarf peas	Golden courgettes
Potatoes	Leeks		Lettuce
	Red kale		Ruby chard

ALTERNATIVE PLANTING

In addition to vegetables and herbs, the ornamental kitchen garden can also include fruit to complement the cane fruit grown around the edge of this potager. Training redcurrants and gooseberries as standards makes picking their fruit easier. 'Ballerina' apples could be planted as an upright screen and 'step-over' apples grown as edging round the beds.

ORNAMENTAL FRUIT

Strawberries in pots or beds

Blueberries in pots

'Ballerina' apple trees

Cape gooseberries

Standard redcurrants

Fan-trained peach

Figs in pots

Autumn-fruiting raspberries

SUNNY ALPINE BED

PLANTS THAT NEED PERFECT DRAINAGE
will thrive in a raised bed filled with gritty
soil in a sunny site. A mulch of coarse grit
will help to keep the 'necks' of the plants
dry and reduce slug damage to spring-
flowering bulbs. The raised position will
suit creeping plants, which can cascade
over the edge, and many will self-seed into
the wall and the paving or bed below. The
walls create shade or shelter that provide
different environments for the plants,
which are shown here in late spring. Curb
the growth of vigorous plants to prevent
more delicate plants being smothered.

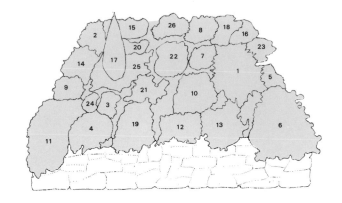

PLANTING GUIDE

1 *Agapanthus* 'Lilliput'

2 *Aurinia saxatilis* 'Citrina'

3 *Antennaria microphylla*

4 *Artemisia schmidtiana* 'Nana'

5 *Campanula cochleariifolia* 'Elizabeth
   Oliver'

6 *Rhodanthemum hosmariense*

7 *Crepis incana*

8 *Daphne cneorum*

9 *Dianthus* 'Pike's Pink'

10 *Diascia cordata*

11 *Dryas octopetala*

12 *Erodium chrysanthum*

13 *Geranium cinereum* 'Ballerina'

14 *Geranium cinereum* var. *subcaulescens*

15 *Helianthemum* 'Rhodanthe Carneum'

16 *Iberis sempervirens* 'Little Gem'

17 *Juniperus communis* 'Compressa'

18 *Linum perenne*

19 *Origanum* 'Kent Beauty'

20 *Oxalis adenophylla*

21 *Primula marginata* 'Linda Pope'

22 *Pulsatilla vulgaris*

23 *Saxifraga* 'Southside Seedling'

24 *Sempervivum arachnoideum*

25 *Thymus serpyllum*

26 *Verbascum* 'Letitia'

ACID-TOLERANT PLANTS IN SHADE

YOU CAN TAILOR THE SOIL in a raised bed to suit the plants you wish to grow, and this scheme, shown in late spring, allows acid-loving plants to be grown in a shady spot even if the garden soil is alkaline. Use wooden or stone edging, avoiding limestone, concrete and mortar, which are alkaline and will seep into the soil.

PLANTING GUIDE

1. *Andromeda polifolia*
2. *Corydalis cashmeriana*
3. *Epigaea gaultherioides*
4. *Gentiana sino-ornata*
5. *Shortia soldanelloides*

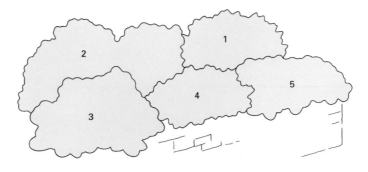

LIME-TOLERANT PLANTS IN SHADE

IF AN ALKALINE SOIL CAN BE KEPT MOIST a wide range of plants can be grown in a raised bed, and this scheme will provide colour through spring. Ramondas are sensitive to damp in the centre of the rosette in winter, and grow better if planted vertically. The iris, soldanella and dicentra will creep over the soil surface.

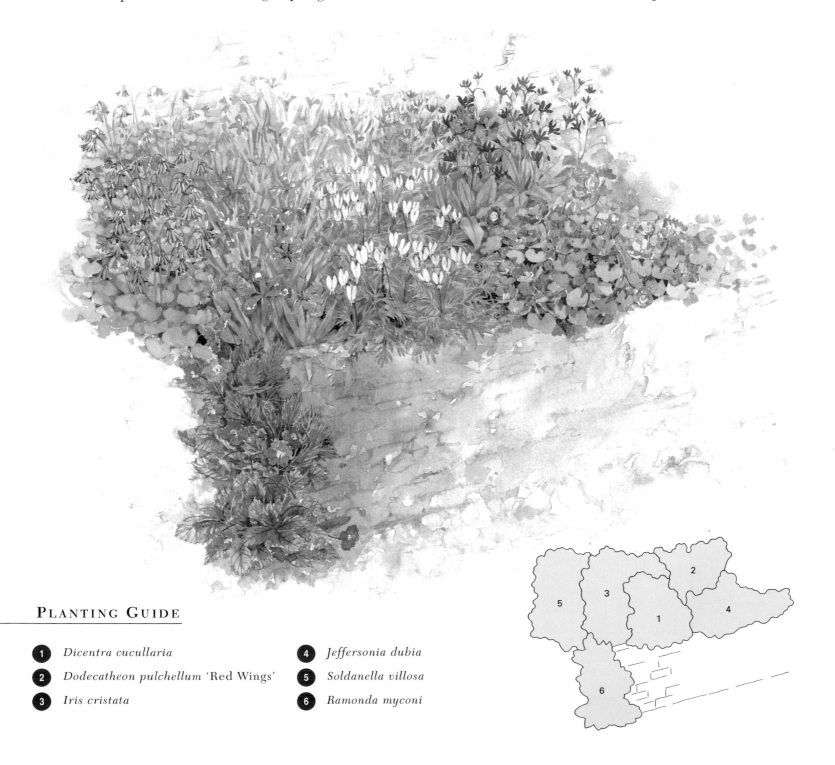

PLANTING GUIDE

1. *Dicentra cucullaria*
2. *Dodecatheon pulchellum 'Red Wings'*
3. *Iris cristata*
4. *Jeffersonia dubia*
5. *Soldanella villosa*
6. *Ramonda myconi*

ACID BED

THE MOIST, ACID CONDITIONS of a peat bed suit many delicate plants. The bed should be positioned in partial shade. It is the diversity of choice plants that is the point of this late-spring scheme, which is planted on a gentle slope terraced with branches. Peat blocks are available, but to reduce the amount of peat used, leafmould from trees on acid soil and composted bark can be mixed with the compost. To prevent birds disturbing dormant crowns in winter, cover the plants with squares of fine chicken wire.

PLANTING GUIDE

1. *Adiantum pedatum*
2. *Adiantum pedatum* var. *subpumilum*
3. *Anemone nemorosa*
4. *Anemone ranunculoides*
5. *Asarum europaeum*
6. *Betula nana*
7. *Cassiope* 'Edinburgh'
8. *Celmisia coriacea*
9. *Corydalis flexuosa*
10. *Cyclamen coum*
11. *Cyclamen purpurascens*
12. *Dodecatheon pulchellum*
13. *Epipactis gigantea*
14. *Erythronium* 'Pagoda'
15. *Gentiana sino-ornata*

16. *Hacquetia epipactis*
17. *Iris cristata*
18. *Jeffersonia dubia*
19. *Lilium formosanum* var. *pricei*
20. *Lilium regale*
21. *Linnaea borealis*
22. *Matteuccia struthiopteris*
23. *Narcissus cyclamineus*
24. *Phlox divaricata*
25. *Primula gracilipes*
26. *Primula vulgaris*
27. *Primula whitei*

28. *Rhododendron cinnabarinum*
29. *Rhododendron* 'Curlew'
30. *Rhododendron williamsianum*
31. *Saxifraga fortunei*
32. *Shortia soldanelloides*
33. *Trillium grandiflorum* 'Flore Pleno'
34. *Trillium rivale*
35. *Trillium sessile*
36. *Uvularia grandiflora*
37. *Vaccinium vitis-idaea* subsp. *minus*

ALTERNATIVE PLANTING

The cool moist conditions in a peat bed are ideal for many Himalayan plants that are not easy to grow in sunny, drier parts of the garden. These include the bizarre flowers and mottled stems of arisaemas, and the fragile beauty of meconopsis. Many of these have beautiful leaves that form attractive rosettes in the years before they produce their large flower spike, set seed and then die.

HIMALAYAN SCHEME

8   *Meconopsis punicea*

12 *Primula nana*

13 *Arisaema consanguineum*

20 *Meconopsis betonicifolia*

26 *Arisaema candidissimum*

33 *Roscoea cautleyoides*

34 *Cautleya spicata* 'Robusta'

36 *Arisaema jacquemontii*

SCREE GARDEN

IN NATURE A SCREE is a constantly moving
soil, covered with a thick layer of stone chips
that gives plants perfect drainage. The plants
tend to have creeping stems that send up new
shoots if the soil level changes, or deep tap
roots to reach moisture. In the garden a scree
is usually sited on the slope of a rock garden
and is planted with alpines that require sun
and dryness at the soil surface. Some of these
late-spring-flowering plants are sensitive to
winter wet and will benefit from a sheet of
glass or plastic placed over them in winter.

PLANTING GUIDE

1. *Acantholimon glumaceum*
2. *Aethionema grandiflorum*
3. *Alyssum montanum*
4. *Androsace sempervivoides*
5. *Anthemis cretica* subsp. *cretica*
6. *Armeria juniperifolia*
7. *Campanula portenschlagiana*
8. *Carlina acaulis*
9. *Dianthus alpinus*
10. *Dianthus erinaceus*
11. *Edraianthus graminifolius*
12. *Erinacea anthyllis*
13. *Genista sagittalis* subsp. *delphinensis*
14. *Gentiana verna*
15. *Gypsophila aretioides*
16. *Gypsophila repens*
17. *Leontopodium alpinum* 'Mignon'
18. *Linum* 'Gemmell's Hybrid'
19. *Morisia monanthos*
20. *Papaver alpinum*
21. *Phlox subulata* 'Marjorie'
22. *Pterocephalus perennis*
23. *Pulsatilla vernalis*
24. *Sempervivum montanum*
25. *Viola cornuta* 'Minor'

SUNNY ROCK GARDEN

ALPINES GROW BEST IN A SUNNY SITE and
will thrive in a raised bed or in a rock garden
where they look more natural. The best time
to plant is in spring or early summer, which is
when this scheme is shown, when the alpines
are in active growth. Rockwork and soil
preparation should be completed in autumn
so that it can settle ready for planting. Aim for
a balance of plants and rock surfaces and put
in the larger, structural plants first.

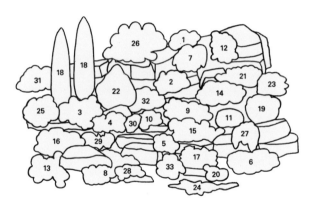

PLANTING GUIDE

1. *Acantholimon glumaceum*
2. *Aethionema* 'Warley Rose'
3. *Aurinia saxatilis* 'Citrina'
4. *Androsace sarmentosa*
5. *Armeria juniperifolia*
6. *Campanula cochleariifolia*
7. *Chiastophyllum oppositifolium*
8. *Cyclamen coum*
9. *Daphne cneorum* 'Eximia'

10. *Dianthus* 'La Bourboule'
11. *Dianthus erinaceus*
12. *Erinus alpinus*
13. *Euphorbia myrsinites*
14. *Euryops acraeus*
15. *Gentiana acaulis*
16. *Iberis sempervirens*
17. *Iris pumila*
18. *Juniperus communis* 'Compressa'

19. *Linum perenne*
20. *Oxalis adenophylla*
21. *Penstemon newberryi*
22. *Picea glauca* var. *albertiana* 'Conica'
23. *Picea mariana* 'Nana'
24. *Pratia pedunculata*
25. *Pulsatilla rubra*
26. *Salix lanata*
27. *Saxifraga* 'Tumbling Waters'

ALTERNATIVE PLANTING

Spring is the season when most rock gardens look their best, but although there are fewer plants that bloom in autumn this scheme can be altered so there is more interest at the end of summer. One of the easiest ways is to plant autumn-flowering bulbs such as crocus and sternbergias, but avoid colchicums, which have huge leaves in spring that die down later and look ugly.

AUTUMN SCHEME

ALPINE LAWN

GRASS IS NOT NEEDED in an alpine lawn, since the ground is covered by a tapestry of low-growing and creeping plants. In this example, which is illustrated at its best in midsummer, thymes create a carpet of aromatic leaves and flowers, studded with other small plants. Most of the plants are prostrate but height is provided by pulsatillas and sisyrinchiums, and festucas make evergreen, contrasting clumps of blue-grey.

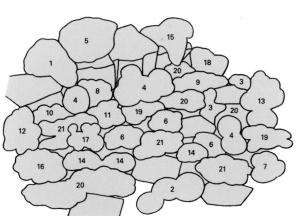

PLANTING GUIDE

1. *Aurinia saxatilis* 'Citrina'
2. *Armeria maritima* 'Vindictive'
3. *Chamaemelum nobile* 'Treneague'
4. *Festuca glauca*
5. *Genista lydia*
6. *Gentiana acaulis*
7. *Helianthemum* 'Rhodanthe Carneum'
8. *Helianthemum* 'Wisley Primrose'
9. *Potentilla cuneata*
10. *Pratia pedunculata*
11. *Pterocephalus perennis*
12. *Pulsatilla vulgaris* var. *rubra*
13. *Pulsatilla vulgaris*
14. *Sagina subulata* var. *glabrata* 'Aurea'
15. *Saxifraga* 'Tumbling Waters'
16. *Scutellaria orientalis*
17. *Sempervivum montanum*

ALTERNATIVE PLANTING

In very dry situations a similar effect can be produced by using sempervivums and sedums, while in mild climates, where frosts are rare, echeverias could also be used. Echeverias have larger rosettes and make a good contrast to the red and green of sempervivums, and they can be used as temporary accent plants in cold climates. The plants will not withstand any treading.

DROUGHT-TOLERANT PLANTS

Sedum acre 'Aureum'

Sedum spathulifolium 'Cape Blanco'

Sedum spathulifolium 'Purpureum'

Sempervivum arachnoideum

Sempervivum arachnoideum var. *bryoides*

Sempervivum 'Atropurpureum'

Sempervivum calcareum

Sempervivum 'Commander Hay'

18   *Sisyrinchium angustifolium*

19   *Thymus serpyllum* var. *albus*

20   *Thymus serpyllum* 'Annie Hall'

21   *Thymus serpyllum coccineus*

CONTAINER GARDENS

GROWING PLANTS IN CONTAINERS HAS MANY ADVANTAGES: POTS CAN BE MOVED AROUND THE GARDEN TO PROTECT PLANTS FROM COLD WEATHER IN WINTER AND THE CULTIVATION OF PLANTS THAT WOULD NOT GROW IN THE GARDEN, SUCH AS LIME-HATING PLANTS, BECOMES POSSIBLE. IN ADDITION THERE IS GREAT SCOPE FOR THE IMAGINATION. BY GROWING PLANTS IN INDIVIDUAL POTS AND GROUPING THEM TOGETHER YOU CAN COMBINE PLANTS THAT SIMPLY WOULD NOT BE GOOD NEIGHBOURS IN THE GARDEN. YOU CAN ALSO BRING PLANTS AT THEIR PEAK INTO THE PICTURE AND REMOVE THEM WHEN THEY ARE PAST THEIR BEST. BUT MORE THAN ANYTHING ELSE, CONTAINER GARDENING IS WORRY-FREE, AND IF A COMBINATION OF PLANTS DOES NOT WORK AS WELL AS YOU HAD HOPED, IT CAN EASILY BE CHANGED, SO YOU CAN BE BOLD WITH PLANTS AND COMBINATIONS AND TAKE A FEW RISKS.

Simple plant combinations have extra charm when grown in ornamental pots. The terracotta provides a linking colour between the pansies and marigolds.

SCHEMES FOR PAVED AREAS

CONTAINERS BRIGHTEN UP paved areas and allow great flexibility. Not only can you mix unusual plants in a single container but plants can be grown in separate pots and arranged and rearranged as the mood suits. Plants can be brought to the front as they reach their peak and then hidden from view as they fade.

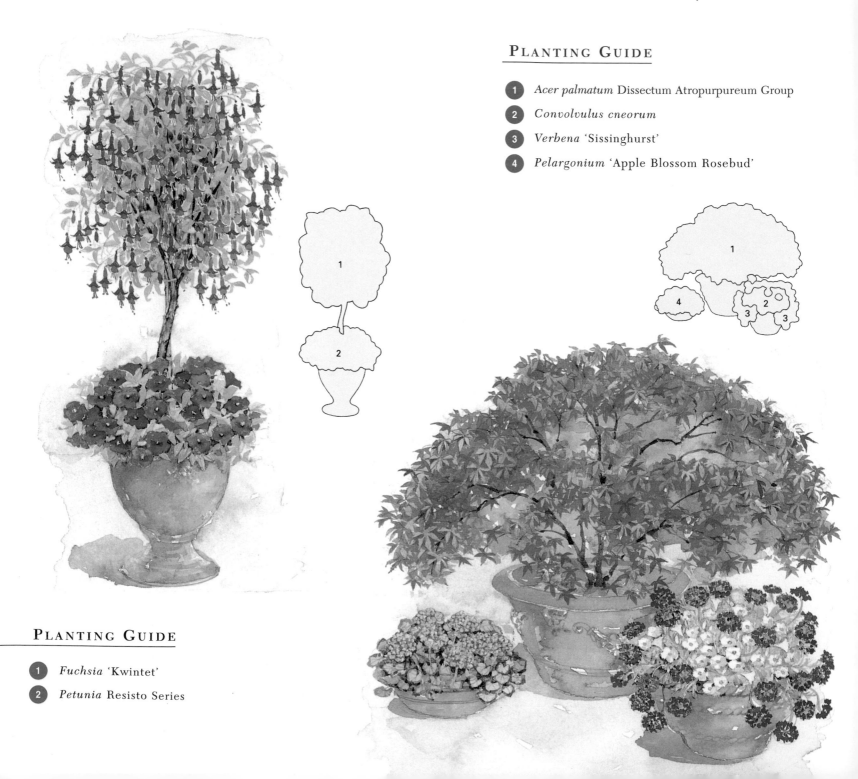

PLANTING GUIDE

1 *Acer palmatum* Dissectum Atropurpureum Group

2 *Convolvulus cneorum*

3 *Verbena* 'Sissinghurst'

4 *Pelargonium* 'Apple Blossom Rosebud'

PLANTING GUIDE

1 *Fuchsia* 'Kwintet'

2 *Petunia* Resisto Series

PLANTING GUIDE

1 *Ilex aquifolium* 'J.C. Vän Tol'

2 *Viola* x *wittrockiana* Universal Series

ALTERNATIVE PLANTING

When planting any permanent plants such as shrubs in containers it is better to use a compost that contains loam. This is heavier than soilless composts so plants are less likely to be blown over, and it contains more nutrients so plants are not so dependent on you to feed them. If some brightness is needed to lighten up a paved area, try these yellow and pink alternatives.

YELLOW AND PINK SCHEMES

LEFT: 1 *Anisodontea capensis*

2 *Diascia barberae* 'Hopleys Apricot'

CENTRE: 1 *Acer shirasawanum* 'Aureum'

2 *Choisya ternata* 'Sundance'

3 *Asteriscus maritimus*

4 *Fuchsia* 'Genii'

RIGHT: 1 *Ilex aquifolium* 'Flavescens'

2 *Viola* x *wittrockiana* Universal Series (yellow)

GROUP PLANTING FOR SUN

THESE THREE POTS are planted for a sunny position and combine seasonal flowers with bold and contrasting foliage. The phormium will naturally maintain the arching habit, but the standard cupressus will need regular clipping to keep it neat and regular. The large leaves of the aralia are divided into small leaflets, each edged with white, and in time it will attain a palm-like habit and produce clouds of small, white flowers in late summer. In autumn the summer bedding can be replaced with polyanthus, pansies and bulbs such as daffodils and dwarf tulips. When planting pots, try to match the shape and colour of the container with the planting.

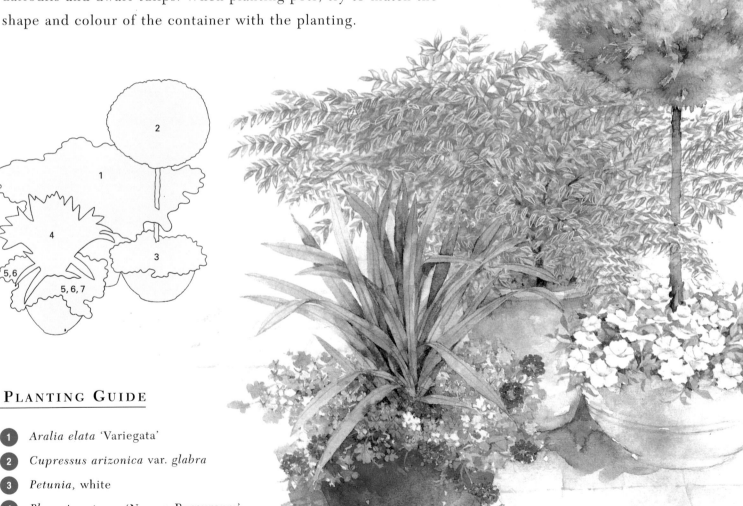

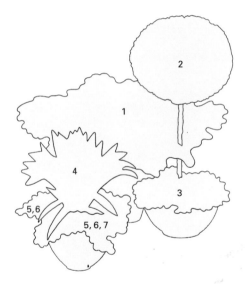

PLANTING GUIDE

1. *Aralia elata* 'Variegata'

2. *Cupressus arizonica* var. *glabra*

3. *Petunia*, white

4. *Phormium tenax* 'Nanum Purpureum'

5. *Pelargonium* 'L'Elégante'

6. *Viola* 'Belmont Blue'

7. *Verbena* x *hybrida* 'Amethyst'

GROUP PLANTING FOR SHADE

THIS SIMPLE GROUP of three plants in three pots contrasts the broad foliage of the hosta with the fine filigree of the fern. The tender begonias bring a different colour to the group. Their shiny leaves also reflect light and contrast in texture with the matt surface of the hosta and the scaly stems of the fern.

PLANTING GUIDE

1. *Hosta fortunei* var. *aureomarginata*
2. *Polystichum setiferum*
3. *Begonia semperflorens*

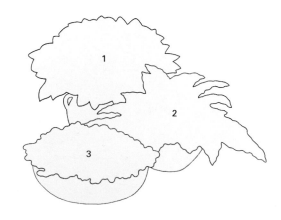

WINTER AND SUMMER WINDOWBOXES

WINDOWBOXES OFFER GREAT design possibilities, especially as they are seen from both outside and inside the house. Some of the most effective schemes have a repeat planting with two or three large plants in a row, a number of medium-sized plants and trailing plants at the front. If they are grown against house walls, with shelter from the cold, tender plants often survive the winter, especially in towns. If plants are replaced twice a year they can provide colour and interest in every month of the year.

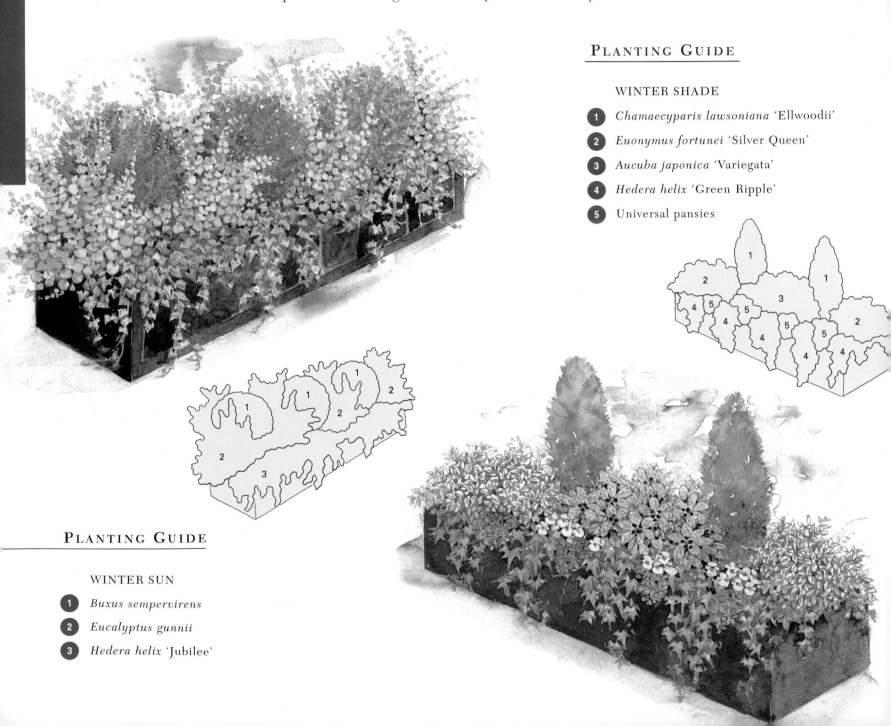

PLANTING GUIDE

WINTER SHADE

1. *Chamaecyparis lawsoniana* 'Ellwoodii'
2. *Euonymus fortunei* 'Silver Queen'
3. *Aucuba japonica* 'Variegata'
4. *Hedera helix* 'Green Ripple'
5. Universal pansies

PLANTING GUIDE

WINTER SUN

1. *Buxus sempervirens*
2. *Eucalyptus gunnii*
3. *Hedera helix* 'Jubilee'

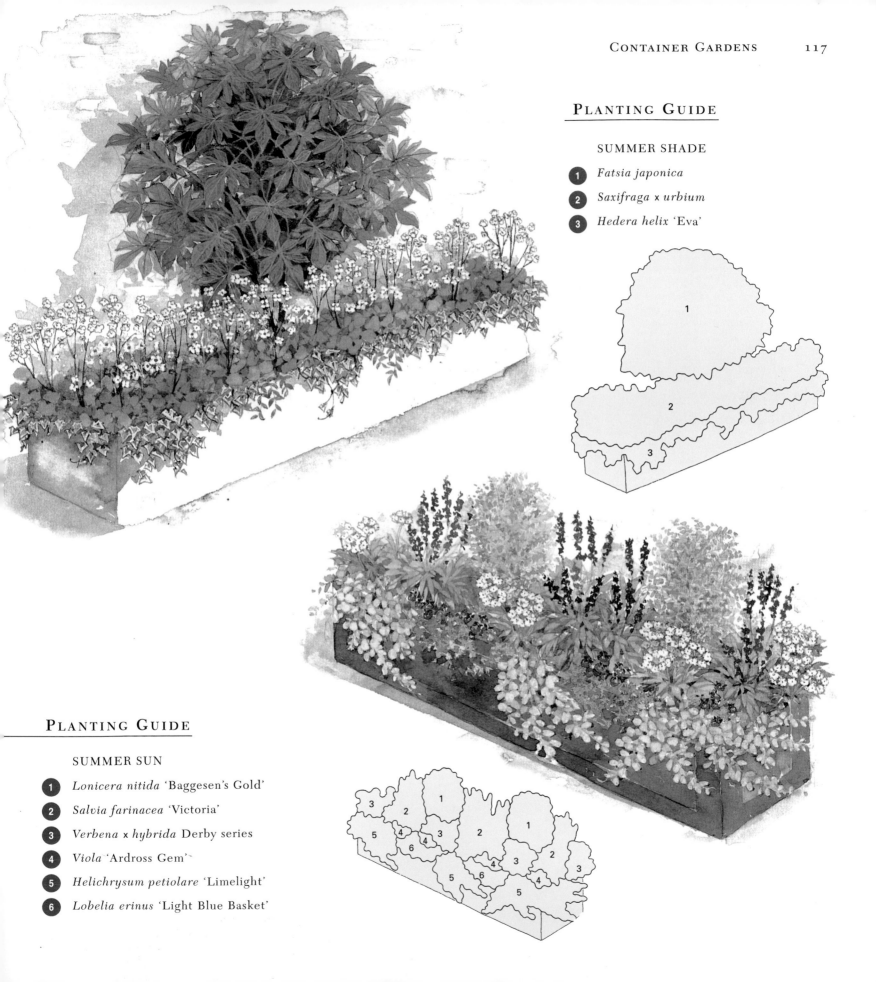

PLANTING GUIDE

SUMMER SHADE

1 *Fatsia japonica*

2 *Saxifraga x urbium*

3 *Hedera helix* 'Eva'

PLANTING GUIDE

SUMMER SUN

1 *Lonicera nitida* 'Baggesen's Gold'

2 *Salvia farinacea* 'Victoria'

3 *Verbena x hybrida* Derby series

4 *Viola* 'Ardross Gem'

5 *Helichrysum petiolare* 'Limelight'

6 *Lobelia erinus* 'Light Blue Basket'

SPRING CONTAINER

MOST GARDENERS PLANT FOR SUMMER but containers can bring spring colour to areas of the garden and beside the house where there is no soil. Choose evergreens for the main components and mix in variegated plants to lighten the display. Creeping alpines such as *Euphorbia myrsinites* and iberis soften the edges of the container and a pastel mix of white tulips, cream daffodils and blue grape hyacinths complete this scheme.

PLANTING GUIDE

1. *Iberis sempervirens*
2. *Juniperus communis* 'Compressa'
3. *Euphorbia myrsinites*
4. *Tulipa* 'Purissima'
5. *Narcissus* 'Thalia'
6. *Muscari armeniacum* 'Blue Spike'
7. *Myosotis* 'Royal Blue'

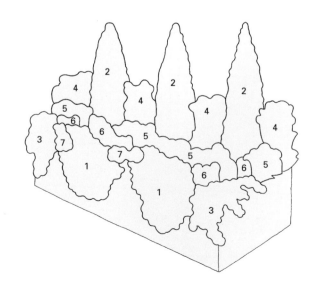

WINTER CONTAINER

SOMETIMES SIMPLICITY IS BEST and this combination of
three evergreens in containers will look as interesting in
winter as it does the rest of the year. The large mound of
pieris dominates the group, and the young leaves are
dramatic in spring but bright throughout the year.
Skimmia forms a deep green mound and in winter
the red flower buds are bright and cheerful
before they open to scented, white flowers. In
contrast, the yellow leaves of box are carried
on upright, wiry branches. For extra colour,
variegated ivy and spring-flowering bulbs
are planted in the containers.

PLANTING GUIDE

1 *Pieris formosa* var. *forrestii* 'Wakehurst'

2 *Hedera helix* 'Glacier'

3 *Skimmia japonica* 'Rubella'

4 *Buxus sempervirens* 'Aureovariegata'

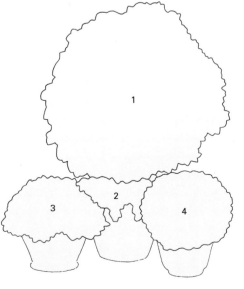

A PEACEFUL CITY RETREAT

THESE SCHEMES ARE planted simply, and the absence of bright colours or strong contrasts of foliage shape and size produces an elegant effect. They combine shrubs and climbers to screen out noise and unwanted views in a town garden and are suitable for a patio or balcony. The use of evergreens means that they look good all year, but when flowers do appear they are clean and white, and most are scented as well.

PLANTING GUIDE

1. *Elaeagnus pungens* 'Maculata'
2. *Vinca minor* 'Atropurpurea'
3. *Viola* 'Jersey Gem'

PLANTING GUIDE

1. *Camellia japonica* 'Alba Simplex'
2. *Lysimachia nummularia* 'Aurea'
3. *Hedera helix* 'Green Ripple'

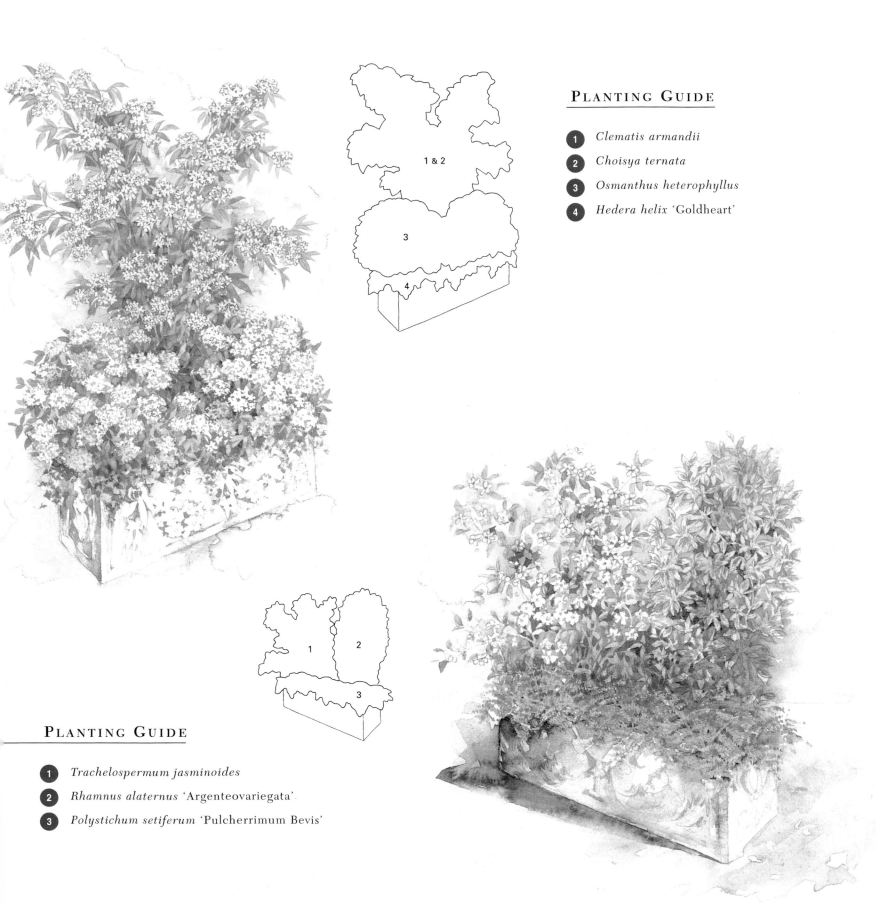

PLANTING GUIDE

1. *Clematis armandii*
2. *Choisya ternata*
3. *Osmanthus heterophyllus*
4. *Hedera helix* 'Goldheart'

PLANTING GUIDE

1. *Trachelospermum jasminoides*
2. *Rhamnus alaternus* 'Argenteovariegata'
3. *Polystichum setiferum* 'Pulcherrimum Bevis'

TROUGHS FOR SUN AND SHADE

ALPINES THRIVE IN TUBS AND TROUGHS and the jewel-like flowers can be appreciated at close quarters. Containers are also easier to weed, and provide early flowers with some protection from slugs and snails. The shady trough (this page) should be filled with a mix of composted bark, leafmould and peat so that, although the compost is well drained, it still holds moisture. These plants include lime-haters, so do not use a concrete or limestone trough. The trough (right) for sun should have a gritty compost with loam. Raising the trough on bricks prevents the drainage holes from becoming blocked.

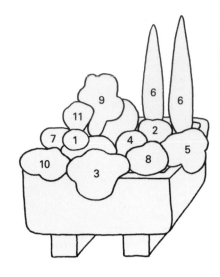

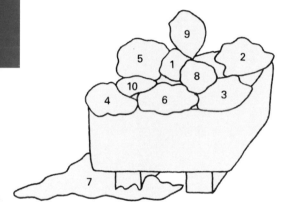

PLANTING GUIDE

1. *Adiantum pedatum*
2. *Asplenium trichomanes*
3. *Cassiope* 'Edinburgh'
4. *Gentiana ternifolia*
5. *Haberlea rhodopensis*
6. *Iris cristata*
7. *Pratia penunculata*
8. *Ramonda myconi*
9. *Olsynium douglasii*
10. *Trillium rivale*

PLANTING GUIDE

1 *Androsace hirtella*

2 *Daphne arbuscula*

3 *Dianthus alpinus*

4 *Gentiana verna*

5 *Globularia repens*

6 *Juniperus communis* 'Compressa'

7 *Oxalis* 'Ione Hecker'

8 *Rhodohypoxis baurii*

9 *Saxifraga cochlearis*

10 *Saxifraga paniculata*

11 *Sisyrinchium* 'E.K. Balls'

ALTERNATIVE PLANTING

In mild areas a container in a sunny situation can
be planted with tender lampranthus and aeoniums.
These succulent plants have distinctive foliage and
attractive flowers in bright shades for long periods.
In colder areas these plants may survive light frost
if kept dry, and if the tub can be moved to a frost-
free greenhouse the plants will flower profusely
the following spring.

TENDER SCHEME

1 *Aeonium arboreum* 'Atropurpureum'

2 *Aeonium haworthii*

3 *Aichryson* x *domesticum* 'Variegatum'

4 *Aptenia cordifolia* 'Variegata'

5 *Lampranthus brownii*

6 *Lampranthus spectabilis* 'Tresco Apricot'

7 *Lampranthus spectabilis* 'Tresco Fire'

8 *Delosperma lehmannii*

PLANT DIRECTORY

THIS PLANT DIRECTORY GIVES DETAILS OF THE PLANTS USED IN THE PLANTING RECIPES IN THIS BOOK. EACH ENTRY GIVES A BRIEF DESCRIPTION OF THE PLANT AND RECOMMENDED SPECIES AND CULTIVARS FOLLOWED BY DETAILS OF THE APPROXIMATE SIZE IT WILL ACHIEVE AND ITS HARDINESS. SYMBOLS INDICATE IF A PLANT IS SUITABLE FOR A SPECIAL PART OF THE GARDEN OR HAS SPECIFIC NEEDS. ARTISTS' ILLUSTRATIONS OF THE PLANTS WILL BE FOUND IN THE BOOK WHERE THEY FORM PART OF THE PLANTING RECIPES AND THEIR EFFECT AND VALUE IN THE GARDEN CAN BE APPRECIATED.

PLANTING KEY

H = height; S = spread

Hardiness 1. Plants require heated glass
Hardiness 2. Plants require unheated glass
Hardiness 3. Plants are hardy in warmer regions or situations, or can be grown outside in summer but need protection from frost in winter
Hardiness 4. Plants are hardy throughout the British Isles and most of Europe

- ☼ sun
- ⛅ semi-shade
- ☁ shade
- ◊ tolerates dry, poor, light soil
- ♦ tolerates heavy, moist,soil
- ✂ regular pruning advisable
- ✂̸ no pruning necessary
- ❀ fragrance
- ✾ bee or butterfly plant

See also back flap of jacket for Planting Key

Abelia x *grandiflora* An evergreen, arching shrub with small, glossy leaves and pale pink, tubular flowers in summer and autumn. H: 2m (6ft) S: 2m (6ft). Hardiness 4 ☼ ◊ ❀ ✂ - spring,

Acaena saccaticupula 'Blue Haze' A creeping, evergreen ground-cover plant with feathery, grey-blue leaves and round, white flowerheads in early summer followed by dark red burrs. H: 15cm (6in) S: 1m (3ft). Hardiness 4 ☼ ◊ ✂̸

Acantholimon glumaceum The prickly mats of narrow leaves grow slowly and are studded with small clusters of pink flowers in summer. Useful perennial for dry soils. H: 8cm (3in) S: 30cm (1ft). Hardiness 4 ☼ ◊ ✂̸

Acanthus These herbaceous perennials make bold clumps in the border, with their architectural foliage and upright flower spikes. *A. mollis* has leaves up to 1m (3ft) long, and white flowers emerging from purple bracts in summer. The Latifolius Group has larger, broad leaves. *A. spinosus* 'Lady Moore' is more compact with arching leaves with spiny margins. H: 1.5m (5ft) S: 1m (3ft). Hardiness 4 ☼ ⛅ ◊ ♦ ✾

Acer palmatum Acers are shrubs or trees with an elegant habit and foliage which usually colours well in autumn. They need neutral or acid soil and protection from wind. Dissectum Atropurpureum Group has purple foliage, turning scarlet in autumn. H: 2m (6ft) S:3m (10ft) 'Orido-Nishiki' has variegated foliage. H: 4m (12ft) S: 3m (10ft). Hardiness 4 ⛅ ✂̸

Achillea These perennials are useful for rock gardens and sunny borders. They have flat heads of tiny flowers in summer, in shades of white, yellow and pink. *A. filipendulina* has grey leaves and tall stems of yellow flowerheads. H: 1.2m (4ft) S: 45cm (18in). *A. millefolium* has white flowers. H: 60cm (2ft) S: 60cm (2ft). *A.* 'Moonshine' has grey leaves and pale yellow flowers. H: 60cm (2ft) S: 60cm (2ft). *A.* 'Taygetea' has grey leaves and branched stems of pale yellow flowers. H: 60cm (2ft) S: 45cm (18in). Hardiness 4 ☼ ⛅ ◊ ✾

Aconitum 'Ivorine' Aconites are tough perennials for the border, usually with deep blue flowers on tall spikes. They are easier to grow than, but look similar to, delphiniums. *A.* 'Ivorine' is bushy and has branched stems of creamy flowers in summer. H: 90cm (3ft) S: 45cm (18in). Hardiness 4 ☼ ⛅ ◊ ♦

Acorus These are useful foliage plants for moist soil with narrow, grass-like leaves. *A. calamus* 'Variegatus' is a deciduous perennial and has white-striped leaves. It will grow in up to 22cm (9in) of water. H: 90cm (3ft) S: 60cm (2ft). *A. gramineus* is much smaller and will grow in water or moist soil. H: 30cm (1ft) S: 15cm (6in). 'Ogon' has cream stripes; 'Variegatus' has yellow stripes. Hardiness 4 ☼ ⛅ ♦

Actinidia These vigorous deciduous climbers are best known as the source of Kiwi fruits (*A. deliciosa*). This species has large leaves with red hairs on the foliage and stems. H: 10m (33ft). *A. kolomikta* has white and pink foliage and needs a sheltered position. H: 5m (16ft). Hardiness 4 ☼ ⛅ ✂ - late winter

Achillea millefolium

Agapanthus Headbourne hybrids

Allium cristophii

Adiantum These ferns have elegant, finely divided foliage on black stems. Some are tender but a few, such as *A. pedatum,* are hardy. Keep out of hot sun. H: 30cm (1ft) S: 30cm (1ft). Hardiness 4

Aethionema This group of dwarf shrubs, good for alkaline soils, bear flowers in late spring, in shades of white, pink and lilac. *A. grandiflorum* is semi-evergreen with pale to deep pink flowers. H: 30cm (1ft) S: 30cm (1ft). *A.* 'Warley Rose' has rich pink flowers. H: 20cm (8in) S: 20cm (8in). Hardiness 4 ☀ ☁ ⋇ - spring

Agapanthus Agapanthus make large clumps of green, strap-like leaves and have round heads of (usually) blue flowers in mid- to late summer. The evergreen perennials with broad leaves are less hardy than those with narrow, deciduous leaves such as *A.* 'Lilliput' – H: 40cm (16in) S: 40cm (16in) – and *A.* Headbourne hybrids – H: 60cm (2ft) S: 60cm (2ft). Hardiness 3–4 ☀

Ajuga reptans This ground-covering herbaceous perennial retains some leaves in winter and bears spikes of blue flowers in early summer. It spreads rapidly and will grow in most soils. There are many ornamental cultivars with coloured leaves,

including 'Atropurpurea', purple, 'Variegata', white-edged, and 'Burgundy Glow' marked in pink and purple. H: 15cm (6in) S: 90cm (3ft). Hardiness 4 ☀ ☁ ⬧ ⋇

Alchemilla mollis A perennial, this is the commonest species of the genus, with round, grey-green leaves covered with silky hairs. In summer, the plumes of tiny lime-green flowers are good for cutting. It self-seeds and can be used in the wild garden and in paving. H: 60cm (2ft) S: 75cm (30in). Hardiness 4 ☀ ☁ ◌ ⬧

Alisma plantago-aquatica This perennial pond plant has rosettes of long, heart-shaped leaves and small, three-petalled, white flowers in summer. It will grow in wet soil or in up to 30cm (1ft) of water. H: 60cm (2ft) S: 45cm (18in). Hardiness 4 ☀ ☁

Allium The ornamental onions range from small alpines such as the deep pink *A. insubricum* to the big drumsticks of *A. hollandicum* and *A. giganteum.* Their foliage is usually tatty at flowering time and should be hidden with other plants. Most prefer sunny, well-drained soil and flower in late spring. *A. cristophii,* silvery lilac H: 60cm (2ft) S: 15cm (6in). *A. hollandicum,* purple H: 90cm (3ft) S: 10cm (4in).

A. hollandicum 'Purple Sensation', deep violet H: 90cm (3ft) S: 10cm (4in). *A. schoenoprasum* (chives) H: 30cm (1ft) S: 30cm (1ft). Hardiness 4 ☀ ◌ ⋇

Alonsoa warscewiczii The deep orange flowers of this tender perennial are carried for many months from the summer on wiry-stemmed, bushy plants. H: 45cm (18in) S: 30cm (1ft). Hardiness 1 ☀ ☁ ◌

Aloysia triphylla Although the flowers of lemon-scented verbena are insignificant, this tender shrub is worth growing for the lemon fragrance of its narrow, rough-textured leaves. It is deciduous and requires a sheltered position to survive outside in frosty areas. It can be grown in pots and moved inside in winter. H: 2m (6ft) S: 2m (6ft). Hardiness 3 ☀ ◌ ⊚

Amaranthus caudatus Some ornamental amaranthus have bright foliage and require sheltered conditions, but *A. caudatus* is a hardy annual that self-seeds in some gardens. Commonly known as love-lies-bleeding, it has crimson tassels of tiny flowers that hang down from the bushy plants. 'Viridis' has deep green tassels that fade to cream as they age. H: 90cm (3ft) S: 50cm (20in). Hardiness 2 ☀ ☁

Amaryllis belladonna The true amaryllis is a bulbous garden plant with rosy-pink or white scented flowers in late autumn. It bears about six funnel-shaped flowers on tall, dark stems before the leaves appear. It requires a sheltered position, and dislikes disturbance. H: 60cm (2ft) S: 10cm (4in). Hardiness 3 ☼ ◊ ✿

Anaphalis triplinervis The leaves of this hardy perennial have three distinctive veins, and they form a mound of grey foliage. Clusters of white, papery flowers appear in late summer. 'Sommerschnee' has brighter white flowers. H: 80cm (32in) S: 60cm (2ft). Hardiness 4 ☼ ☁ ◆

Andromeda polifolia This evergreen, dwarf shrub is suitable for acid, but not dry, soils. It has small urn-shaped flowers in shades of pink or white in spring and late summer. H: 40cm (16in) S: 60cm (2ft). Hardiness 4 ☼ ☁

Androsace Most of the 100 species of androsace form tight rosettes with short-stemmed flowers in shades of pink or white in late spring. They require sun and well-drained soil. *A. cylindrica* x *hirtella* and *A. sempervivoides* are evergreen perennials with pink flowers. H: 5cm (2in) S: 20cm (8in). *A. sarmentosa* forms mats of loose rosettes and clusters of pink flowers. H: 10cm (4in) S: 30cm (1ft). Hardiness 4 ☼ ◊

Aponogeton distachyos

Anemone This large genus includes alpines, herbaceous plants and 'bulbs'. Most flower in spring and have poppy-like flowers. *A. blanda* has blue flowers in early spring. H: 15cm (6in) S: 15cm (6in). Japanese anemones (*A. hupehensis*, *A* x *hybrida*, *A. tomentosa* and *A. vitifolia*) flower in late summer, in shades of pink and white. H: 1m (3ft) S: 60cm (2ft). *A. narcissiflora* has clusters of white flowers above a ruff of bracts. H: 40cm (16in) S: 45cm (18in). *A. nemerosa* has delicate, white flowers in spring. H: 15cm (6in) S: 30cm (1ft). *A. ranunculoides* has bright yellow flowers in spring. H: 15cm (6in) S: 30cm (1ft). Hardiness 4 ☼ ☁ ☁

Anemonopsis macrophylla This elegant woodland perennial has coarse foliage and almost black stems with nodding pink flowers in late summer. H: 75cm (30in) S: 45cm (18in). Hardiness 4 ☁ ☁ ◆

Antennaria microphylla (*A. dioica* var. *rosea*) The thin, prostrate stems of this semi-evergreen perennial are covered with silver leaves and form low, spreading mats for the rock garden or in paving. The clusters of pink flowers appear in spring. H: 5cm (2in) S: 45cm (18in). Hardiness 4 ☼ ◊

Anthemis Most have finely divided foliage and large daisy flowers, in shades of white or yellow. They are summer-flowering perennials for the rock garden or border. *A. cretica* (*A. montana*) is dwarf with white flowers. H: 15cm (6in) S: 30cm (1ft). *A. tinctoria* has many cultivars, with flowers in yellow shades. H: 90cm (3ft) S: 90cm (3ft). Hardiness 4 ☼ ◊ ✿

Anthriscus sylvestris 'Ravenswing' Although the common cow parsley is not welcome in most gardens, this biennial cultivar, with deep purple foliage is a striking contrast to other garden plants. It will seed itself in most gardens and grows true from seed. H: 1m (3ft) S: 45cm (18in). Hardiness 4 ☼ ◆ ✿

Anthyllis montana In late spring the silky leaves of this sun-loving perennial are almost hidden under the globular heads of pink flowers. It thrives in dry soil in full sun. H: 30cm (1ft) S: 60cm (2ft). Hardiness 4 ☼ ◊ ✿

Aponogeton distachyos Often called water hawthorn because of the appearance and smell of the flowers, this perennial pond plant has floating leaves and will grow in water 60cm (2ft) deep. It is evergreen in mild areas. Hardiness 3 ☼ ☁

Aquilegia Most aquilegias are short-lived perennials for the rock garden or border with elegant foliage and nodding, long-spurred flowers in early summer. *A. alpina* has blue and white flowers. H: 45cm (18in) S: 30cm (1ft). *A. canadensis* has spidery blooms in scarlet and yellow. H: 9 cm (3ft) S: 30cm (1ft). *A. vulgaris* is the common columbine in purple and pink. 'Nivea' is white. H: 90cm (3ft) S: 45cm (18in). Hardiness 4 ☼ ☁

Aralia elata 'Variegata' In winter the gaunt, stiff branches of this small tree look strange, but in summer the finely divided, large leaves, edged with white, make this a handsome plant. In late summer clouds of white, fluffy flowers are produced. H: 5m (15ft) S: 5m (15ft). Hardiness 4 ☼ ☁

Arbutus unedo Although this will eventually become a tree, it is usually seen as a large shrub because of its slow growth. It is an evergreen flowering plant that will tolerate alkaline soil and coastal conditions and the white flowers are produced in autumn as the red, edible but bland, fruit ripen. The fruit gives the plant its common name of strawberry tree. H: 8m (25ft) S: 6m (20ft). Hardiness 4 ☼ ☁ ◊

Arenaria balearica The carpeting, almost moss-like growth is studded with small, white flowers in summer. It will creep over rocks and paving in moist places, making an evergreen mat. H: 1cm (½in) S: 30cm (1ft). Hardiness 4 ☼ ☁

Argyranthemum These small, tender shrubs are popular as bedding plants in temperate areas and are grown for their daisy-like flowers in shades of pink, white and yellow which are produced over a long period. *A. foeniculaceum* has very fine grey leaves and white flowers. *A.* 'Jamaica Primrose' is pale yellow and *A.* 'Vancouver' is pink. H: 1m (3ft) S: 1m (3ft). Hardiness 3 ☼ ◊

Arbutus unedo

Aruncus dioicus

Armeria These tussock-forming perennials have narrow, grass-like leaves and rounded heads of pink or white flowers in early summer. They are suitable for rock gardens, and edging in full sun. *A. juniperifolia* is very compact. H: 8cm (3in) S: 15cm (6in). *A. maritima* H: 15cm (6in) S: 30cm (1ft). Hardiness 4 ☼ ◊

Artemisia Some artemisias are considered weeds, some are herbs, but most have attractive, fine, silvery foliage. Most are hardy in dry soils and are herbaceous or low shrubs that are best pruned in early spring to cut out old growth. They have little beauty in flower. *A. alba* 'Canescens' has wiry foliage. H: 45cm (18in) S: 30cm (1ft). *A. absinthium* has grey leaves. H: 1m (3ft) S: 60cm (2ft). *A. arborescens* is an upright shrub with feathery leaves. H: 1m (3ft) S: 1.5m (5ft). *A.* 'Powis Castle' is woody with fine foliage. H: 60cm (2ft) S: 1m (3ft). *A. schmidtiana* 'Nana' is a compact, silvery-green plant. H: 8cm (4in) S: 30cm (1ft). *A. stelleriana* is a creeping plant with coarsely divided, silver leaves. H: 15cm (6in) S: 45cm (18in). Hardiness 4 ☼ ◊ ⊗ ⋏ - spring

Arum These exotic-looking tuberous perennials have large, glossy leaves and distinctive flowers with a broad spathe and

upright spadix. *A. creticum* has showy, creamy flowers in spring and attractive leaves. H: 30cm (1ft) S: 20cm (8in). Hardiness 3 ☼ ◊ *A. italicum* 'Marmoratum' has white-veined foliage through winter and red berries in late summer (toxic). H: 30cm (1ft) S: 15cm (6in). Hardiness 4 ☼ ☁ ◖

Aruncus dioicus This bold, herbaceous plant has coarsely divided foliage, and cream, feathery plumes of tiny flowers in summer. It will tolerate dry conditions better than the rather similar astilbes. H: 2m (6ft) S: 1.2m (4ft). Hardiness 4 ☼ ☁ ◊ ◖

Arundo donax This giant grass with grey-green leaves is evergreen in mild climates but requires winter protection in cold areas. The variegated form is spectacular as a foliage plant but more tender. Autumn plumes of purple flowers are produced in mild climates. H: 4m (13ft) S: 1.5m (5ft). Hardiness 3 ☼ ◖

Asarum europaeum The evergreen glossy, rounded leaves of this creeping woodland perennial is its main attraction although the strange, liver-coloured, three-pointed flowers are interesting, but rather hidden. The leaves have a spicy smell when crushed. It prefers moist acid or neutral soil. H: 8cm (3in) S: 30cm (1ft). Hardiness 4 ☁ ☁

Asclepias tuberosa The curious, orange flowers of this perennial are carried above stiffly upright stems of bright green leaves in late summer. Hybrids have a wider colour range. Irritant sap. H: 1m (3ft) S: 30cm (1ft). Hardiness 4 ☼ ◊ ✿ ⊗

Asparagus Although considered a luxury, asparagus is easy to grow if the soil is well drained and enriched with compost. A bed will crop for many years when established.

Asplenium These ferns include the hart's tongue fern (*A. scolopendrium*). *A. trichomanes* has delicately divided foliage with black stems and is often seen on dry-stone walls. H: 15cm (6in) S: 20cm (8in). *A. ceterach* has lobed fronds with brown scales on the reverse. H; 15cm (6in) S: 20cm (8in). Hardiness 4 ☼ ☁

Aster The perennial asters include Michaelmas daisies and they are valuable for late summer colour. *A.* x *frikartii* 'Mönch' has lilac flowers for many months. H: 70cm (28in) S: 45cm (18in). *A. novae-angliae* has clusters of flowers in a wide colour range, mildew-resistant H: average 1m (3ft) S: 45cm (18in). *A. thomsonii* 'Nanus' produces lilac flowers for a long period. H: 60cm (2ft) S: 30cm (1ft). Hardiness 4 ☼ ◖ ⊗

Astilbe In moist, acid soils these perennials are essential for their feathery plumes of flowers in shades of white, pink and red. They are good for cutting and the dead flowers are attractive in the garden in winter. *A. chinensis* var. *pumila* is dwarf with reddish leaves and dumpy spikes of deep pink flowers. H: 25cm (10in) S: 20cm (8in). *A. chinensis* var. *taquetii* 'Purpurlanze' will tolerate more drought than most and has purple flowers. H: 1.2m (4ft) S: 1m (3ft). Hardiness 4 ☼ ☁ ◖

Astrantia Perfect in cottage gardens, these perennials have long stems of small flowers with colourful bracts above mounds of coarse foliage. They thrive in most soils and are good for cutting. *A. carniolica* var. *rubra* has deep pink flowers. *A. major* subsp. *involucrata* 'Shaggy' has long bracts. *A. major* 'Sunningdale Variegated' has pink flowers and white-edged leaves. *A. major rosea* has pink

flowers. *A major rubra* has deep pink flowers.
A. major 'Hadspen Blood' has beetroot-red
flowers. H: 75cm (30in) S: 45cm (18in).
Hardiness 4 ☀ ☁ ◖

Athyrium niponicum var. *pictum* The
Japanese painted fern is more colourful than
most with purple and silver-flushed leaves
and purple stems. It prefers moist, acid,
woodland soils, shade and some shelter. H: 30cm
(1ft) S: 30cm (1ft). Hardiness 4 ☁ ☁

Atriplex Although they have little merit in
flower, the leaves of the various atriplex can
be attractive. *A. halimus* is an evergreen
shrub with silver leaves. H: 2m (6ft) S: 2m
(6ft). *A. hortensis* var. *rubra* is a hardy annual
with deep red foliage. H: 2m (6ft) S: 60cm
(2ft). Hardiness 4 ☀ ◊

Aucuba Aucubas grow well in dense shade,
but they also thrive in sunny places, where
they make a more compact shrub. The
variegated forms are most common.
A. japonica 'Rozannie' has male and female
flowers on the same plant so produces good
crops of red berries. H: 1m (3ft) S: 1m (3ft).
Hardiness 4 ☀ ☁ ☁ ◊ ◖

Aurinia saxatilis (*Alyssum saxatile*) This is a
common plant on rockeries. The dwarf,
evergreen perennial produces masses of
small, mustard-yellow flowers in late spring,
lemon-yellow in 'Citrina'. H: 20cm (8in)
S: 30cm (1ft). Hardiness 4 ☀ ◊

Azara microphylla 'Variegata' The tiny leaves
of this evergreen shrub are bordered with
white, but in spring the vanilla-scented, fluffy
orange flowers are the main attraction. It
makes a good wall shrub. H: 10m (30ft) S: 4m
(13ft). Hardiness 4 ☀ ☁ ☁ ⊗

Azolla mexicana This floating aquatic fern
makes a feathery carpet, but can be invasive
in small, warm pools. In autumn the light
green fronds change to crimson. H: 1cm
(½in). Hardiness 3 ☀ ☁

Ballota pseudodictamnus Although it has a
woody base, this subshrub is best cut back
hard each spring to keep it as a compact
mound of soft, rounded, grey-green leaves. In

Berberis thunbergii 'Atropurpurea'

Bergenia 'Silberlicht'

late spring small flowers are produced in the
centre of persistent, greyish, funnel-shaped
calyces along the ends of the shoots. H: 45cm
(18in) S: 60cm (2ft). Hardiness 4 ☀ ◊

Begonia semperflorens The common bedding
begonia is useful because it will grow in light
shade and flowers continually all summer in
cool climates, and all year where winters are
frost-free. Although perennial it is usually
treated as an annual. Cultivars with bronze or
green leaves are available and flowers range
from white through pink to red. Double
forms are propagated by cuttings. H: 30cm
(1ft) S: 20cm (8in). Hardiness 3 ☀ ☁

Bellis perennis The common lawn daisy has
double-flowered forms that bring colour to
the garden in spring. Most are grown from
seed, but perennial forms should be divided
regularly. 'Prolifera' is the hens-and-chickens
daisy with tiny flowers around the main
bloom. H: 15cm (6in) S: 15cm (6in).
Hardiness 4 ☀ ☁ ◖

Berberis Spines are the common attribute of
berberis, which includes evergreens, shrubs
with bright autumn colour, spring flowers and
showy berries. Most are easy to grow and
tolerant of a wide range of conditions.
B. temolaica is deciduous, with white stems

and red berries in autumn. H: 2m (6ft) S: 3m
(10ft). *B. thunbergii* is deciduous with bright
autumn colour. H: 1m (3ft) S: 1m (3ft).
B. thunbergii f. *atropurpurea* has purple
foliage in summer. H: 1m (3ft) S: 1m (3ft).
Hardiness 4 ☀ ☁ ☁ ◊ ◖ ⚘

Bergenia These evergreen perennials are
valued for their large, glossy leaves and
bright spring flowers. The Ballawley Hybrids
have red foliage in winter and deep pink
flowers. *B. ciliata* has hairy leaves and is
rather tender. *B. cordifolia* has deep pink
flowers and red-tinged leaves in winter.
B. purpurascens has purple flowers and red-
tinged leaves in winter. *B.* 'Silberlicht' has
white flowers. *B.* 'Sunningdale' has lilac-
magenta flowers and red leaves in winter.
H: 40cm (16in) S: 60cm (2ft). Hardiness 4
☀ ☁ ◖

Beta vulgaris Common beet has been
developed into beetroot and Swiss chard
which is attractive in its cultivars with red
and yellow leaf stalks.

Betula Birches tolerate poor soils and are
hardy. They are also of varied habit although
the trees are more common than the dwarfer,
bushy kinds. *B. nana* is a spreading shrub
with yellow autumn colour. H: 60cm (2ft)

S: 2m (6ft). *B. pendula* is the common silver birch with white bark on mature plants. H: 25m (80ft) S: 10m (30ft). Hardiness 4 ☼ ◊ ◗

Blackberry The common blackberry (*Rubus fruticosus*) is useful in cold areas where spring blossom can be damaged by frost. Plants are large and spiny; some are thornless.

Borago officinalis An annual or biennial herb with bristly leaves and branched stems of blue, star-shaped flowers in summer. The blooms have a cucumber flavour and are used as a garnish in salads and drinks. H: 60cm (2ft) S: 30cm (1ft). Hardiness 4 ☼ ◊ ✿

Brachyglottis 'Sunshine' Better known as *Senecio greyii*, this low shrub has spreading growth and rounded leaves of greyish green. The bright yellow daisy flowers can be removed before they open in summer. H: 1m (3ft) S: 1.5m (5ft). Hardiness 4 ☼ ◊

Brassica oleracea This plant has been developed into cabbages, Brussels sprouts and cauliflower. All prefer heavy, alkaline soil and require full sun.

Brunnera The forget-me-not-like flowers of this perennial are carried on airy sprays above the clumps of bold, heart-shaped foliage during early summer. Brunnera is vigorous enough to survive in the wild garden but neat enough for borders in sun or shade. *B. macrophylla* has hairy leaves and soft blue flowers. 'Hadspen Cream' has creamy-white leaf edges. Aluminium Spot ('Langtrees') has silvery spots on the leaves. H: 45cm (18in) S: 60cm (2ft). Hardiness 4 ☼ ◌ ◗

Buddleja Few shrubs are as popular as the butterfly bushes, in particular *B. davidii* which has cultivars in pink, red, purple and white. There are also more unusual species with small, scented flowers. *B. alternifolia* flowers in early summer, with lilac blooms. H: 4m (13ft) S: 4m (13ft). ✂ - after flowering. *B. crispa* has woolly leaves and lilac flowers in autumn. H: 3m (10ft) S: 3m (10ft). ✂ - spring. *B. fallowiana* var. *alba* has white-felted leaves and white flowers. H: 2m (6ft) S: 3m (10ft) ✂ - spring. Hardiness 4 ☼ ◊ ✿ ✿

Buglossoides purpurocaerulea The intense blue flowers of this perennial are produced in late spring and early summer. It requires rich, moist, acid or neutral soil and a sunny position with some protection from the midday sun and drought. H: 60cm (2ft) S: 60cm (2ft). Hardiness 4 ☼ ☁

Bupleurum fruticosum This evergreen shrub has deep green, glossy leaves, and clusters of small, yellow flowers in late summer. It is especially suitable for seaside gardens and may be damaged in cold climates. H: 2m (6ft) S: 2.5m (8ft). Hardiness 4 ☼ ◊ ✂ spring

Butomus umbellatus The flowering rush will grow as a marginal or with up to 25cm (10in) of water above the crown. In summer the rush-like foliage is augmented by umbels of pink, starry flowers. H: 1.5cm (5ft) S: 45m (18in). Hardiness 4 ☼

Buxus sempervirens Box has dense evergreen foliage that makes it perfect for clipping into low hedges and topiary. Many cultivars have variegated foliage. Box will grow in most soils including alkaline ones. 'Aureovariegata' has yellow variegated foliage. 'Elegantissima' has leaves outlined with white. 'Suffruticosa' is the dwarf box. H: 1.5m (5ft) S: 1.5m (5ft). Hardiness 4 ☼ ☁ ☁ ◊ ◗ ✂

Calamintha nepeta The lesser catmint has hairy, aromatic leaves. It is a low-growing, bushy perennial with clusters of pink or mauve flowers in summer. H: 45cm (18in) S: 45cm (18in). Hardiness 4 ☼ ☁ ◊ ✿ ✿

Calendula officinalis The wild species is rarely grown, but there are many cultivars with flowers in shades of cream, orange and yellow from summer to autumn. It is a hardy annual that will survive most winters and self-seed. The leaves are fragrant and the flowers can be used in cosmetics and salads. H: 45cm (18in) S: 30cm (1ft). Hardiness 4 ☼ ◗ ✿

Calla palustris This marginal pond plant has glossy, heart-shaped leaves, white 'arum' flowers in summer and clusters of red berries in autumn. It will grow in up to 25cm (10in) of water. It is good for medium-sized pools

and scrambles over moist soil and into the water. May cause skin irritation. H: 20cm (8in) S: 60cm (2ft). Hardiness 4 ☼

Caltha palustris The perennial marsh marigold has clusters of bright yellow flowers in spring, followed by coarse, shiny, rounded leaves. It thrives in boggy soil or very shallow water. *Caltha palustris* 'Flore Pleno' is larger in all its parts. H: 40cm (16in) S: 60cm (2ft). Hardiness 4 ☼ ☁

Camellia In acid soils camellias are an essential part of spring and their glossy evergreen foliage is attractive all year. These plants flower better in sun than in shade, but avoid east-facing positions. They are ideal for tubs but must not be allowed to dry out. *C. japonica* 'Alba Simplex' has white, single flowers with a few pink specks. H: 4m (13ft) S: 3m (10ft). Hardiness 4 ☼ ☁

Campanula Despite the huge range, from towering herbaceous plants to delicate alpines, most campanulas can be recognized by their bell-shaped flowers. They are usually blue or white, but some, such as the biennial Canterbury bells, are pink. *C. cochleariifolia* is a dwarf alpine with pale blue flowers. 'Elizabeth Oliver' has double flowers. H: 8cm (3in) S: 30cm (1ft). *C. glomerata* is a spreading border plant with purple flowers. H: 30cm (1ft) S: 60cm (2ft). *C. latiloba* has saucer-shaped, blue flowers, mauve in

Caltha palustris

'Hidcote Amethyst'. H: 90cm (3ft) S: 45cm (18in). *C. persicifolia* double blue is the peach-leaved bellflower. H: 90cm (3ft) S: 30cm (1ft). *C. pyramidalis* is a tall biennial. H: 2m (6ft) S: 30cm (1ft). *C. portenschlagiana* is a vigorous creeping perennial with sprays of blue flowers. H: 15cm (6in) S: 45cm (18in). *C. rapunculus* is a coarse plant for the wild garden. H: 60cm (2ft) S: 60cm (2ft). *C. rotundifolia* is a wiry alpine with blue bells. H: 15cm (6in) S: 15cm (6in). Hardiness 4 ☼ ◊

Canna indica 'Purpurea' The bold leaves of cannas bring an exotic feel to the garden, and although tender perennials they are easy to keep over the winter. The summer flowers of the many hybrids are showy, in shades of red, pink, yellow and orange, but *C. indica* 'Purpurea' has small flowers and is grown principally for its purple leaves. H: 1.5m (5ft) S: 60cm (2ft). Hardiness 3 ☼

Cardamine Cardamines are useful perennials for the woodland garden with clusters of small, four-petalled flowers in shades of white, lilac or pink in late spring. *C. pratensis* is a plant for moist soil and for wild gardens, with lilac flowers but the double form 'Flore Pleno' is more attractive. H: 45cm (18in) S: 30cm (1ft). *C. raphanifolia* is a spreading perennial with pink or white flowers. H: 60cm (2ft) S: 60cm (2ft). *C. trifolia* is a compact plant with deep green leaves and white flowers. H: 15cm (6in) S: 30cm (1ft). Hardiness 4 ☼ ☁ ✹

Carex The sedges are grass-like plants with a wide variety of habits and there are many variegated sorts that tolerate average or moist soils. The base of the leaves is usually triangular in cross-section. *C. elata* 'Aurea' is a deciduous plant with golden foliage. H: 60cm (2ft) S: 45cm (18in). *C. pendula* is a coarse plant making large tufts of green leaves and long, arching stems of drooping flower spikes. H: 1.2m (4t) S: 1.5m (5ft). Hardiness 4 ☼ ☁ ●

Carlina acaulis This dwarf thistle is as attractive when dead, in winter, as in summer. It is a short-lived perennial that forms small clumps of low, prickly leaves and almost

stemless, large thistle flowers up to 10cm (4in) across, in silver and gold shades. H: 10cm (4in) S: 30cm (1ft). Hardiness 4 ☼ ◊ ✹

Carpenteria californica This slightly tender shrub is an evergreen that flowers in mid-summer. The glossy, deep green leaves contrast with the pure white, gold-centred, poppy-like flowers. H: 2m (6ft) S: 2m (6ft). Hardiness 4 ☼ ◊ ✤ ✗– spring

Caryopteris x *clandonensis* In late summer the fragrant foliage of this dwarf shrub is covered with small clusters of feathery, blue flowers. There are several cultivars available including 'Dark Knight' with silver foliage and deep blue flowers and 'Worcester Gold' which has yellow leaves and blue flowers. H: 1m (3ft) S: 1m (3ft). Hardiness 4 ☼ ◊ ✗– spring ✤ ✹

Cassiope The upright branches and scale-like leaves of these acid-loving shrubs look like a dwarf conifer, but in late spring the white, bell-shaped flowers show them to be related to heathers. They are dainty plants for cool parts of the rock garden and woodland. *C.* 'Edinburgh' is a good, upright plant. H: 25cm (10in) S: 25cm (10in) Hardiness 4 ☁ ✗

Carpenteria californica

Ceanothus There are two groups of ceanothus; the evergreen shrubs flower in spring and have blue flowers, and the deciduous kinds have looser clusters of flowers, in late summer, in pale blue, white and pink. *C.* 'Burkwoodii' is a bright blue evergreen. H: 1.5m (5ft) S: 2m (6ft). *C.* x *delineanus* 'Gloire de Versailles' has pale blue flowers. H: 1.5m (5ft) S: 1.5m (5ft). *C. impressus* is a spreading evergreen with blue flowers. H: 1.5m (5ft) S: 2.5m (8ft). *C. thyrsiflorus* var. *repens* is a creeping evergreen. H: 1m (3ft) S: 2.5m (8ft). Hardiness 3–4 ☼ ◊ ✤

Celmisia coriacea Celmisias have perennial rosettes of silver, narrow leaves and bold, large, white, daisy flowers in late spring. They prefer acid, humus-rich, well-drained soil. *C. coriacea* makes bold clumps. H: 40cm (16in) S: 40cm (16in). Hardiness 4 ☼ ☁

Centaurea *C. cyanus* is the annual blue cornflower. *C. montana* is a spreading perennial with large, spidery, blue flowers. There are also purple-flowered natives such as *C. scabiosa*, H: 60cm (2ft) S: 30cm (1ft), and *C. nigra*, H: 60cm (2ft) S: 30cm (1ft). Hardiness 4 ☼ ☁ ◊ ✹

Centranthus ruber This perennial, which often seeds into walls and paving, forms large, woody-based clumps with glossy leaves and domed heads of small flowers in white and pink from late spring into summer. *C. ruber atrococcineus* has deep crimson flowers. H: 1m (3ft) S: 1m (3ft). Hardiness 4 ☼ ☁ ◊ ● ✤

Ceratostigma willmottianum The beauty of this small shrub is the display of bright blue flowers in late summer, as its leaves are changing to crimson. It is ideal at the foot of sunny walls and as an edging plant. H: 1m (3ft) S: 1.5m (5ft). Hardiness 4 ☼ ◊ ●

Chaenomeles The Japanese quince has colourful flowers in spring and useful fruit in autumn. It tolerates a variety of soils and can be used as a wall plant, a shrub or a spiny hedge. *C.* x *superba* has large flowers over a long season. Cultivars include dark-red flowered 'Crimson and Gold' and dark pink 'Pink Lady'. H: 1.5m (5ft) S: 2m (6ft). Hardiness 4 ☼ ☁ ◊ ●

Chaerophyllum hirsutum 'Roseum' This perennial has upright stems of pink, lacy flowers in spring and early summer, and feathery leaves. H: 60cm (2ft) S: 30cm (1ft). Hardiness 4 ☼ ☁ ◗ ✖

Chiastophyllum oppositifolium This mat-forming, succulent alpine has evergreen leaves and long stems of pendulous, small, yellow flowers in late spring. H: 20cm (8in) S: 30cm (1ft). Hardiness 4 ☁ ◊

Choisya ternata This evergreen shrub has fragrant leaves and small, scented, white flowers in spring and in autumn. Sundance has bright yellow leaves. H: 2m (6ft) S: 2m (6ft). Hardiness 4 ☼ ☁ ◊ ◗ ⊛ ✗ - spring.

Chrysogonum virginianum This creeping woodland perennial spreads by runners and has small, single, yellow blooms in summer. The leaves are hairy and heart-shaped. H: 25cm (10in) S: 60cm (2ft). Hardiness 4 ☼ ☁

Cimicifuga racemosa Cimicifugas are late-flowering perennials that form large, long-lived clumps of coarsely divided leaves. In late summer they produce long, stiff stems with terminal spires of fluffy white or cream flowers. *C. racemosa* has white flowers. H: 1.5m (5ft) S: 60cm (2ft). Hardiness 4 ☼ ☁ ◗

Cistus These sun-loving shrubs thrive in dry soils. Although the silky flowers are short-lived, they are produced in large numbers in summer and the leaves often have a pleasant, resinous scent. *C.* x *aguilarii* has green leaves and white flowers H: 1.2m (4ft) S: 1.2m (4ft). *C.* x *hybridus* has deep green leaves and white flowers. H: 1m (3ft) S: 1.5m (5ft). *C.* x *purpureus* has dark leaves and deep pink flowers. H: 1m (3ft) S: 1m (3ft). *C.* 'Silver Pink' has pale pink flowers. H: 75cm (30in) S: 1m (3ft). Hardiness 4 ☼ ◊ ⊛ ✖ ✗ - spring

Clematis Most clematis prefer a sunny spot with their roots in shade, and well-drained soil. They tolerate alkaline conditions. *C. alpina* 'Frances Rivis' has nodding blue flowers in spring. H: 3m (10ft). *C. armandii* is evergreen and flowers in early spring. H: 5m (16ft). *C. flammula* has masses of tiny cream flowers in late summer. H: 6m (20ft).

Clematis alpina 'Frances Rivis'

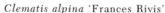

C. 'Jackmanii' has purple flowers in late summer. H: 3m (10ft). *C.* 'Little Nell' has nodding blooms in late summer. H: 2m (13ft). *C.* 'Perle d'Azur' has mid-blue flowers in late summer. H: 3m (10ft). *C. rehderiana* has small cream flowers in late summer. H: 6m (20ft). *C.* 'Etoile Rose' has tubular pink flowers in summer. H: 2m (6ft). Hardiness 4 ☼ ☁

Clerodendrum trichotomum This spreading small tree or large shrub has two seasons of interest. In summer it has clusters of white, starry flowers and in autumn, turquoise berries and red calyces. It is quite fast-growing in a sheltered position. H: 5m (16ft) S: 5m (16ft). Hardiness 4 ☼ ◊ ⊛ ✗ spring

Convallaria majalis Lily-of-the-valley is a useful creeping perennial for shade with spikes of white, bell-shaped flowers in late spring. There are also cultivars with pink flowers and variegated leaves. H: 20cm (8in) S: 30cm (1ft). Hardiness 4 ☼ ☁ ◗ ⊛

Convolvulus cneorum Some convolvulus are considered weeds, but this evergreen shrub with narrow, silver leaves is a well-behaved plant. In late spring the rounded bush is studded with white, funnel-shaped flowers. H: 60cm (2ft) S: 1m (3ft). Hardiness 3 ☼ ◊ ✗ - spring

Convallaria majalis

Cordyline australis In mild areas and in coastal gardens this palm-like plant becomes a narrow tree. In cold gardens it may be cut back to ground level in winter or grown in a pot and protected from frost in winter. Purpurea Group has purple leaves. H: 5m (16ft) S: 1.5m (5ft). Hardiness 3 ☼ ◊

Coreopsis Coreopsis include annuals and perennials, often with woody bases, and yellow flowers in summer. *C. auriculata* has hairy stems and bright gold flowers. H: 80cm (32in) S: 60cm (2ft). *C. lanceolata* has glossy leaves and upright stems with single, yellow flowers. H: 60cm (2ft) S: 45cm (18in). Hardiness 4 ☼ ✖

Coronilla valentina In sheltered gardens this is a pretty, fast-growing evergreen shrub with neat blue-green leaves. In winter and early spring the bush is covered with clusters of scented, yellow flowers. It thrives against a sunny wall. H: 1.5m (5ft) S: 1.5m (5ft). Hardiness 3 ☼ ◊ ⊛ ✗ - spring

Corydalis Most corydalis are small, fleshy herbaceous plants, some tuberous, that flower in spring. They have finely divided leaves and, from late spring, clusters of tubular flowers in shades of yellow, white, pink or blue. *C. cashmeriana* has blue flowers and needs a cool moist spot. H: 25cm (10in) S: 15cm (6in). *C. flexuosa* has blue flowers and is dormant in summer. H: 30cm (1ft) S: 20cm (8in). *C. lutea* is an easy plant that self-seeds in paths and walls. H: 30cm (1ft) S: 30cm (1ft). *C. ochroleuca* has fine foliage and white flowers. H: 30cm (1ft) S: 30cm (1ft). Hardiness 4 ☀ ☁ ◊

Corylus avellana 'Contorta' This slow-growing shrub is a talking point in the garden: although the puckered leaves of the contorted hazel have no great merit in summer, the twisted bare branches are ornamental in winter. H: 5m (16ft) S: 5m (16ft). Hardiness 4 ☀ ☁ ● ✂ – spring

Cosmos atrosanguineus This tuberous perennial is rather floppy and needs to be staked. It then produces its dark maroon flowers, which smell of cocoa, all summer. H: 75cm (30in) S: 45cm (18in). Hardiness 3 ☀ ☁ ☙

Cotinus coggygria Smoke bushes have fluffy plumes of tiny pink flowers in late summer and spectacular scarlet and crimson autumn colour. Plants can be left to grow into small trees, or pruned for larger foliage, but then flowers will not be produced. *C. coggygria* 'Royal Purple' has purple foliage all summer. H: 5m (16ft) S: 5m (16ft). Hardiness 4 ☀ ☁ ● ✂ summer or spring. (irritant sap)

Crocosmia 'Lucifer'

Cotoneaster From ground-covering shrubs to small trees, cotoneasters are easy to grow, with clusters of small, white or pink flowers in early summer and berries in autumn. They may be deciduous or evergreen. *C. franchetii* is an evergreen small tree with red berries. H: 3m (10ft) S: 3m (10ft). *C. microphyllus* is a mounded, evergreen shrub with deep pink berries. H: 1m (3ft) S: 1.5m (5ft). Hardiness 4 ☀ ☁ ◊ ● ✾

Cotula coronopifolia This is a short-lived, succulent perennial for moist soil and pond edges with scented leaves and small, globular heads of yellow flowers. H: 15cm (6in) S: 30cm (1ft). Hardiness 4 ☀ ☁ ●

Crambe maritima This seaside perennial also thrives in inland gardens in well-drained soil. It has large, ruffled, blue-grey leaves and domes of small white flowers in summer. H: 75cm (30in) S: 60cm (2ft). Hardiness 4 ☀ ◊

Crepis incana Many crepis are considered weeds, with yellow, dandelion-like flowers, but *C. incana* is a clump-forming perennial with hairy, grey leaves and showy pink flowers in late summer. H: 30cm (1ft) S: 30cm (1ft). Hardiness 4 ☀ ◊

Crocosmia These clump-forming perennials have upright, grassy leaves and branched stems of trumpet-shaped flowers in shades of yellow, orange and scarlet in summer. They prefer rich, moist soil, mild climates and are good for cutting. *C.* 'Firebird' is bright orange H: 80cm (32in) S: 15cm (6cm). *C.* 'Lucifer' is vigorous and scarlet. H: 1.2m (4ft) S: 15cm (6in). Hardiness 4 ☀ ●

Crocus The popular Dutch crocus has large flowers in yellow, white and purple but there are other species in different colours. *C. chrysanthus* cultivars have goblet-shaped flowers in early spring in a range of bright and pastel colours. 'Gipsy Girl' is yellow with purple stripes. 'Skyline' is blue. H: 8cm (3in) S: 5cm (2in). Hardiness 4 ☀ ☁ ◊ ☙

Cucumber To grow long, spineless cucumbers a greenhouse is required in cool climates, but outdoor ridge cucumbers have more flavour and are easier to grow.

Cupressus arizonica var. *glabra* This is a columnar, evergreen, coniferous tree with blue-grey leaves and reddish bark on mature trees. It is an excellent specimen tree and will tolerate dry soil conditions. It will withstand regular clipping. H: 10m (33ft) S: 4m (13ft). Hardiness 4 ☀ ◊ ✂

Cyclamen These tuberous perennial plants have attractive leaves which are often marbled with grey and are present during winter, and delicate flowers in autumn, winter or spring. Most prefer partial shade. *C. coum* flowers in winter with bright pink blooms. *C. hederifolium* produces its pink flowers in autumn before the leaves appear for the winter. *C. purpurascens* has scented, pink flowers in late summer. H: 10cm (4in) S: 15cm (6in). Hardiness 4 ☀ ☁ ◊ ☙

Cymbalaria muralis This creeping perennial will invade rock gardens and must be planted where it will not be a nuisance. Then it will be admired for its small, glossy leaves and long display of small purple flowers. H: 5cm (2in) S: 60cm (2ft). Hardiness 4 ☀ ☁ ◊

Cynara cardunculus Scolymus Group The cardoon is a dramatic herbaceous plant with arching, deeply cut, silvery foliage and tall stems of large, thistle-like flowerheads that open to deep purple from early summer. It thrives in well-drained soil. H: 2m (6ft) S: 1.2m (4ft). Hardiness 4 ☀ ◊ ✾

Cynoglossum nervosum This bushy perennial has bristly, bright green leaves and upright stems. In early summer the bright blue flowers are produced. It dislikes heavy soils and flowers best in sun on poor or dry soils. H: 60cm (2ft) S: 60cm (2ft). Hardiness 4 ☀ ◊

Cytisus The brooms are fast-growing, colourful shrubs for sunny sites. They are often short-lived but can be kept neater by pruning out flowered shoots as soon as they have faded. *C. battandieri* has silvery, silky leaves and stout spikes of pineapple-scented flowers in early summer. It is slightly tender. H: 5m (16ft) S: 5m (16ft). *C.* 'Zeelandia' is a bushy, rounded shrub with pink and cream flowers in early summer. H: 1.5m (5ft) S: 1.5m (5ft). Hardiness 4 ☀ ◊ ☙ ✂

Dactylorhiza elata hybrid

Dahlia 'Bishop of Llandaff'

Dactylorhiza elata This is a terrestrial (ground-living) orchid that forms clumps of narrow leaves, sometimes spotted with purple. In early summer the spikes of small, deep purple flowers appear and make a vibrant display. This is a choice plant for the border in moist, humus-rich soil. H: 60cm (2ft) S: 15cm (6in). Hardiness 4 ⛅

Dahlia 'Bishop of Llandaff' Dahlias are tuberous perennials valued for their bright flowers, in a wide variety of shapes and colours, over a long period in late summer. This cultivar has widely branched stems with single, bright red flowers and finely cut, deep red foliage, and makes a good plant for the mixed border. H: 1m (3ft) S: 60cm (2ft). Hardiness 3 ☼

Daphne Daphnes are grown for their clusters of small, fragrant flowers that may be white, pink, yellow or green. Some have attractive (toxic) berries. Most prefer neutral soil and all resent being moved. *D. arbuscula* is a dwarf evergreen shrub with pink flowers in early summer. H: 15cm (6in) S: 45cm (18in). *D. bholua* is semi-evergreen with pink flowers in late winter. H: 2m (6ft) S: 1.5m (5ft). *D. cneorum* is a low evergreen with pink flowers. H: 15cm (6in) S: 2m (6ft). *D. laureola* is an evergreen for shade with

green flowers in late winter. H: 1m (3ft) S: 1.5m (5ft). *D. odora* is a slightly tender evergreen with white flowers in spring. H: 1.5m (5ft) S: 1.5m (5ft). Hardiness 3–4 ☼ ⛅ ❀ ✳

Darmera (*Peltiphyllum*) *peltata* This pondside perennial has large rounded leaves on long stalks after the tall stems of domed, pink, flowerheads in spring have faded. The leaves have bright autumn colour. It creeps by thick rhizomes on the surface. H: 1.5m (5ft) S: 1.5m (5ft). Hardiness 4 ☼ ⛅ ♦ ✂

Daucus carota The wild carrot attracts bees and pollinating insects. It is a biennial with flat heads of small white flowers. H: 1m (3ft) S: 30cm (1ft). Hardiness 4 ☼ ♦ ❀

Dianthus Pinks have been bred by gardeners for their fragrance and colourful flowers but the wild species have their own charm. They thrive in dry, alkaline soils and are short-lived, though easily propagated. Most flower in early summer and all are evergreen. *D. alpinus* has single pink flowers in summer. H: 8cm (3in) S: 15cm (6in). *D. caryophyllus* is the carnation and represented by seed selection and cultivars in gardens. *D.* 'Doris' is a popular salmon-pink double. H: 30cm (1ft) S: 30cm (1ft). *D. erinaceus* forms tight cushions with small pink flowers. H: 5cm

(2in) S: 20cm (8in). *D.* 'Fair Folly' has magenta and white flowers. H: 15cm (6in) S: 15cm (6in). *D. gratianopolitanus* is the Cheddar pink with pink flowers. H: 15cm (6in) S: 40cm (16in). *D.* 'La Bourboule' has single pink flowers. H: 8cm (3in) S: 15cm (6in).*D.* 'Musgrave's Pink' has single, white flowers. H: 20cm (8in) S: 15cm (6in). *D.* 'Pike's Pink' has double pink flowers. H: 15cm (6in) S: 15cm (6in). Hardiness 4 ☼ ♦ ❀

Diascia These slightly tender perennials are useful for the rock garden and containers, making spreading or bushy, small-leaved plants. They have spikes of twin-spurred flowers in summer in shades of pink or white. *D. cordata* has deep pink flowers. H: 15cm (6in) S: 15cm (6in). *D.* 'Ruby Field' has salmon-pink flowers. H: 25cm (10in) S: 60cm (2ft). Hardiness 4 ☼ ⛅ ♦ ✿

Dicentra The pendulous, locket-like flowers of dicentras are distinctive, and the most popular is *D. spectabilis* with heart-shaped deep pink and white flowers on arching stems in summer. They are woodland perennials and prefer humus-rich, moist soil. *D. cucullaria* is a choice plant with white flowers – dormant in summer. H: 20cm (8in) S: 30cm (1ft). *D. formosa* forms mats of ferny leaves and pink flowers. H: 45cm (18in) S: 60cm (2ft). Hardiness 4 ☼ ⛅

Dictamnus albus var. *purpureus* This exciting perennial forms clumps of divided leaves and spikes of showy mauve flowers in summer. On hot days volatile oil around the plant can be ignited without harming the plant, giving the name of burning bush. May cause skin irritation. H: 75cm (30in) S: 60cm (2ft). Hardiness 4 ☼ ♦

Digitalis Foxgloves are tall perennials or biennials with rosettes of foliage and spires of pendent, tubular flowers. Most thrive in sun or partial shade and may self-seed in gardens. Toxic. *D. grandiflora* is a clump-forming short species with cream flowers. H: 1m (3ft) S: 45cm (18in). *D. purpurea* has purple flowers but has been bred into mixed colours and the pure white form *albiflora*. H: 1.5m (6in) S: 45cm (18in). Hardiness 4 ☼ ⛅ ❀

Dodecatheon These small, herbaceous perennials are called shooting stars because their pendent, reflexed flowers turn skywards. They flower in late spring and most have white or pink blooms. *D. pulchellum* has stems with up to 20 deep pink flowers. *D.* 'Red Wings' has magenta flowers. H: 30cm (1ft) S: 20cm (8in). Hardiness 4 ☼ ☁ ●

Dryas octopetala This is a low-growing evergreen, alpine shrub that forms creeping mats. In spring it produces white, rose-like flowers followed by fluffy seedheads. H: 10cm (4in) S: 75cm (30in). Hardiness 4 ☼ ◊

Dryopteris Most of these ferns are deciduous and hardy, with upright, 'shuttlecock' forms. They associate well with border plants and most are easy to grow in moist soil in partial shade. There are many ornate cultivars. *D. affinis* has scaly, golden midribs on its fronds. H: 1m (3ft) S: 75cm (30in). *D. dilatata* has brown midribs. H: 1m (3ft) S: 75cm (30in). *D. filix-mas* has green midribs. H: 1m (3ft) S: 75cm (30in). Hardiness 4 ☁ ☁ ●

Eccremocarpus scaber This fast-growing climber clings with tendrils and has bright orange, red or yellow tubular flowers in summer. It is evergreen in mild climates but may be killed in cold areas, where it should be grown as a half-hardy annual. H: 3m (10ft). Hardiness 3 ☼ ◊ ⚔ – spring

Echeveria secunda Echeverias are frost-tender succulents with fleshy rosettes of leaves and tubular red and yellow flower spikes in late spring. They are good foliage plants and in cold climates can be bedded out or grown in pots. *E. secunda* has clumps of grey rosettes. H: 5cm (2in) S: 30cm (1ft). Hardiness 3 ☼ ◊

Echinacea In summer the deep pink flowers of these bristly, upright, herbaceous perennials attract butterflies. *E. purpurea* is the most common species. The elegant *E. pallida* is taller and has pendulous petals. H: 1.2m (4ft) S: 60cm (2ft). Hardiness 4 ☼ ◊ ✱

Echinops The globe thistles have coarse, bold foliage, edged with spines and often white underneath. In summer they produce

Eccremocarpus scaber

Erythronium 'Pagoda'

round heads of small flowers in shades of white or blue that attract bees. *E. ritro* is a perennial with blue flowers in late summer. 'Veitch's Blue' has a long season. H: 1m (3ft) S: 45cm (18in). Hardiness 4 ☼ ☁ ◊ ✱

Edraianthus graminifolius This herbaceous perennial is related to campanulas and has similar blue bells. It has clumps of narrow leaves and upright flowers in midsummer. It is a plant for dry sites and rock gardens, and prefers alkaline soil. H: 15cm (6in) S: 15cm (15in). Hardiness 4 ☼ ◊

Eichhornia crassipes In tropical climates this floating aquatic can become a weed, but in temperate gardens it is a novelty with swollen leaf bases and large, lavender flowers in summer. It requires protection from frost. H: 30cm (1ft). Hardiness 3 ☼

Elaeagnus The evergreen species are valued for their silver young growth and variegated cultivars. The small flowers are in late summer or autumn are fragrant. *E.* x *ebbingei* is upright and vigorous with flowers in autumn. 'Limelight' has leaves with yellow centres. H: 3m (10ft) S: 3m (10ft). *E. pungens* 'Maculata' has dark green leaves with butter-yellow centres. H: 2m (6ft) S: 2.5m (8ft). Hardiness 4 ☼ ☁ ◊ ⊚ ⚔ – spring

Epigaea gaultherioides This choice plant requires a humus-rich, acid soil, a sheltered position and partial shade to thrive. It is a low, evergreen shrub with leathery, dark green leaves and bell-shaped, pale pink flowers in spring. H: 10cm (4in) S: 30cm (1ft). Hardiness 4 ☁ ●

Epimedium These spreading, low-growing perennials are popular as ground cover. Their leaves often become bronze in winter and their new growth can be red-tinted. The delicate spring flowers range from white to red and yellow. *E.* x *versicolor* 'Neosulphureum' has pale yellow flowers and is evergreen. ⚔ -spring H: 30cm (1ft) S: 30cm (1ft). Hardiness 4 ☼ ☁ ●

Epipactis gigantea This American, hardy orchid is grown for its spires of greenish-yellow flowers in early summer. It forms clumps of broad leaves and thrives in moist but well-drained soil. H: 45cm (18in) S: 75cm (30in). Hardiness 4 ☁ ☁

Erigeron These hardy annuals or perennials are rather like dwarf Michaelmas daisies and flower in summer. Most have daisy-like flowers in shades of white, lavender, purple and pink. *E. glaucus* has blue-green leaves and mauve and yellow flowers. H: 30cm (1ft)

S: 45cm (18in). *E. karvinskianus* is slender and will self-seed in paving. H: 25cm (10in) S: 75cm (30in). Hardiness 4 ☀ ☁ ✿

Erinacea anthyllis This is a dense, spiny, evergreen shrub for dry sites. In early summer the mounds are studded with pale violet, pea-shaped flowers. H: 30cm (1ft) S: 75cm (30in). Hardiness 4 ☀ ◊

Erinus alpinus This dwarf, evergreen perennial will grow and spread in dry soil and in gravel paths. It flowers in early summer with masses of small pink or lilac blooms. H: 8cm (3in) S: 15cm (6in). Hardiness 4 ☀ ◊

Eriophorum angustifolium In moist soil and in shallow water in ponds, the cotton grass is attractive in summer with its fluffy seed-heads. It is an evergreen with grassy leaves that spreads rapidly. H: 45cm (18in) S: 75cm (30in). Hardiness 4 ☀

Erodium These perennials look like hardy geraniums but the flowers often have two upper petals with markings. Most require well-drained soil and full sun and are neat perennials for a border edge or rock garden. *E. chrysanthum* forms mounds of silvery leaves and pale yellow flowers in summer. H: 15cm (6in) S: 40cm (16in). *E. pelargoniiflorum* is shrubby with large pink and white flowers in summer. H: 30cm (1ft) S: 30cm (1ft). Hardiness 4 ☀ ◊

Eryngium These statuesque perennials have cone-shaped flower clusters surrounded by spiny bracts and are popular for cutting and drying. The perennial species have long tap roots and the biennials self-seed. *E. giganteum* is biennial with green leaves and white bracts. H: 1m (3ft) S: 30cm (1ft). *E. x oliverianum* forms clumps with branched stems of silver flowers. H: 1m (3ft) S: 45cm (18in). *E. x tripartitum* has branched stems of many, small, blue flowers. H: 75cm (30) S: 50cm (20in). Hardiness 4 ☀ ◊ ✿

Erysimum This genus now includes the bedding wallflower but also many small, short-lived, evergreen shrubs that flower in early summer. Many have scented flowers. They have a longer life if grown in poor, dry

soil, but can be propagated by cuttings. *E.* 'Bowles' Mauve' has grey foliage and mauve, scentless flowers all summer. H: 75cm (30in) S: 60cm (2ft). *E. cheiri* 'Harpur Crewe' has bright yellow, double flowers. H: 30cm (1ft) S: 75cm (30in). Hardiness 4 ☀ ◊ ✿

Erythronium These woodland perennials have long, tooth-like bulbs and flower in spring with elegant, reflexed blooms. Many have mottled foliage and flowers can be pink, yellow or white. They require moist, humus-rich soil and semi-shade. *E. dens-canis* has mottled foliage and pink flowers. H: 15cm (6in) S: 10cm (4in). *E.* 'Pagoda' has up to 10 yellow flowers on its branched stems. H: 30cm (1ft) S: 10cm (4in). Hardiness 4 ☁

Escallonia These evergreen shrubs with small, glossy leaves and pink or white flowers in summer are good for hedges, especially in coastal areas. They are fast-growing and not fussy about soil. *E.* 'Donard Seedling' has pink flowers. H: 2.5m (8ft) S: 2.5m (8ft). *E.* 'Red Elf' has deep red flowers. H: 2.5m (8ft) S: 4m (13ft). Hardiness 4 ☀ ◊ ✂ - spring or summer

Eucalyptus In mild areas these fast-growing trees are useful evergreens. *E. gunnii* can be kept as a shrub by pruning each spring, or left to grow into a tree with white flowers in late summer. H: 25m (80ft) S: 15m (50ft). Hardiness 4 ☀ ◊ ✂ - spring

Eucomis bicolor Known as pineapple lily, this bulb forms a clump of leaves and a stout stalk of cream and maroon flowers topped by a tuft of green leaves in late summer. Its distinctive habit makes it popular in mild climates. It needs protection from frost. H: 45cm (18in) S: 20cm (8in). Hardiness 3 ☀

Euonymus The spindle bushes include deciduous species with colourful fruits and autumn colour, and evergreen shrubs. The latter are adaptable and have variegated cultivars that are bright in winter. *E. fortunei* can be used as a shrub or wall plant and is good in coastal areas. 'Canadale Gold' and 'Emerald 'n' Gold' have yellow variegation. H: 60cm (2ft) (more as a climber) S: 1m (3ft). Hardiness 4 ☀ ☁ ☁ ◊ ✂ spring or summer

Eupatorium These are valuable herbaceous perennials for their fluffy flowers in late summer that attract bees and butterflies. They have strongly upright stems and prefer moist soil in sun. They are ideal for wild gardens. *E. cannabinum* has divided leaves and pink or white flowers. H: 1.5m (1ft) S: 1.2m (4ft). *E. purpureum* subsp. *maculatum* has purple stems and pink flowers. H: 2.2m (7ft) S: 1m (3ft). Hardiness 4 ☀ ☁ ● ✿

Euphorbia This large genus of plants includes shrubs, succulents and herbaceous plants. Only the herbaceous species and dwarf shrubs are hardy in frosty climates. The flowers of euphorbias are small but the bracts are often colourful. Their sap is irritant. *E. amygdaloides* var. *robbiae* is good evergreen ground cover. H: 60cm (2ft) S: 75cm (30in). *E. characias* subsp. *wulfenii* is an evergreen shrub with blue-green leaves and lime-green flowers in spring. H: 1.2m (4ft) S: 1.2m (4ft). *E. dulcis* 'Chameleon' is herbaceous with purple foliage. H: 30cm (1ft) S: 30cm (1ft). *E. myrsinites* has creeping stems with grey leaves. H: 10cm (4in) S: 30cm (1ft). *E palustris* is a bushy plant for moist soil with yellow flowers in early summer. H: 1m (3ft) S: 1m (3ft). *E. polychroma* 'Major' has acid yellow flowers in spring. H: 30cm (1ft) S: 75cm (30in). Hardiness 4 ☀ ◊ ●

Eucomis bicolor

Euryops acraeus In sunny, mild gardens this small evergreen shrub forms a dense mound of silver, finely divided foliage. In early summer the gold, daisy flowers open. It requires a well-drained soil and sun. H: 30cm (1ft) S: 30cm (1ft). Hardiness 4 ☼ ◊

Fatsia japonica This evergreen shrub has bold, hand-shaped leaves that are leathery and glossy. In late summer branched heads of globular, white flower clusters are produced. In mild areas it will survive in the garden but requires a sheltered spot. It is also grown as a houseplant. H: 2m (6ft) S: 2m (6ft). Hardiness 3-4 ☼ ⌣ ✬

Filipendula These perennials have white or pink flowers in fluffy heads on upright stems above coarsely divided foliage. *F. ulmaria* prefers moist soil and the golden-leaved cultivar needs partial shade. H: 1m (3ft) S: 60cm (2ft). *F. vulgaris* prefers a drier soil and has fine leaves and white or pale pink flowers. H: 60cm (2ft) S: 45cm (18in). Hardiness 4 ☼ ⌣ ◊ ◗ ✿

Foeniculum vulgare 'Purpureum' This is the herb fennel in its more attractive, purple-leaved form. It is a useful screening plant with tall stems, but young foliage is most attractive. In late summer the tiny yellow flowers attract insects. H: 2m (6ft) S: 45cm (18in). Hardiness 4 ☼ ◊ ✿ ✬

Forsythia This is one of the most common shrubs for spring display and can be covered in bright yellow flowers early in the season. In summer the plants can be dull, with ordinary, green leaves, and little autumn colour. Different cultivars can be chosen for walls or as dwarf shrubs and *F.* 'Fiesta' is variegated. *F.* x *intermedia* 'Spring Glory' is compact with bright flowers. H: 1.2m (4ft) S: 1m (3ft). Hardiness 4 ☼ ◊ ◗ ✄ - spring

Fragaria vesca 'Variegata' This ornamental, variegated form of the ordinary strawberry is a useful perennials for covering soil in sun or semi-shade, though it will not form a dense ground cover to suppress weeds. The leaves are marked with green, grey and white and the flowers are white. H: 15cm (6in) S: 75cm (30in). Hardiness 4 ☼ ⌣

Fritillaria meleagris Fritillaries are bulbous plants with nodding flowers, often in sombre shades, and marked with intricate patterning. Most flower in late spring and are suitable for borders or rock gardens. *F. meleagris* is the snake's head fritillary and has dull purple flowers in late spring. It prefers moist soil and will thrive in grass. *F. meleagris alba* has white flowers. H: 30cm (1ft) S: 8cm (3in). Hardiness 4 ☼ ⌣ ◗

Fuchsia In mild climates fuchsias can become large shrubs but where winter frosts are common require protection. They vary in habit and flower size and colour. *F.* 'Kwintet' has deep pink flowers. *F. magellanica* 'Versicolor' has greyish leaves, small flowers and is hardier than most. *F.* 'Thalia' has deep purple leaves and tubular orange flowers. *F.* 'Tom Thumb' is compact with mauve and carmine flowers. H: up to 2m (6ft) S: up to 2m (6ft). Hardiness 3 ☼ ⌣ ✄ - spring

Galanthus nivalis There are dozens of cultivars and species of snowdrop, with subtle but distinct variations, but the common snowdrop and its double form are perfect for naturalizing in grass, borders and woodland. H: 10cm (4in) S: 10cm (4in). Hardiness 4 ☼ ⌣

Galium Some *Galium* species – with their straggly stems with whorls of narrow leaves and massed, tiny, starry flowers – are invasive and annual weeds, but in wild areas they are useful plants that spread vigorously. The perennial *G. odoratum* has a vanilla scent and white flowers. H: 45cm (18in) S:1m (3ft). *G. verum* has yellow flowers. H: 75cm (30in) S: 1m (3ft). Hardiness 4 ☼ ⌣ ◊ ✿ ✬

Galtonia candicans The summer hyacinth makes a bold display. From strong tufts of broad leaves grow tall spikes with up to 30, bell-shaped flowers of creamy white. It prefers well-drained, fertile and moist soil in sun. In cold areas mulch the bulbs to protect from frost. H: 1.2m (4ft) S: 10cm (4in). Hardiness 4 ☼ ⌣

Garrya elliptica This hardy, evergreen shrub has dark leaves with undulate edges, and long, grey catkins in late winter. Male plants have the best catkins and 'James Roof' is a

popular cultivar. Garrya will thrive on a shady wall but will be damaged by cold winds. H: 4m (12ft) S: 4m (12ft). Hardiness 4 ☼ ⌣ ⚥ - spring

Gaultheria procumbens This genus now includes the berrying plants formerly known as pernettyas (*G. mucronata*) and they are all lime-hating evergreen shrubs grown for their foliage, small summer flowers and bright berries. *G. procumbens* is a creeping plant whose leaves smell of wintergreen, and scarlet berries. H: 15cm (6in) S: 1m (3ft). Hardiness 4 ☼ ⌣

Genista Brooms give masses of yellow flowers at various times of the year. Most grow and flower quickly from seed, but some are short-lived. *G. sagittalis* subsp. *delphinensis* is a low, deciduous shrub flowering in spring. H: 15cm (6in) S: 30cm (1ft). *G. hispanica* is a bushy, spiny, dwarf shrub that flowers in early summer. H: 75cm (30in) S: 1.5m (5ft). *G. lydia* is a low, arched shrub flowering in early summer. H: 60cm (2ft) S: 1m (3ft). Hardiness 4 ☼ ◊ ✿ ⚥ - after flowering.

Gentiana Gentians are popular alpine perennials. *G. acaulis* makes low mats of bright green leaves and stemless deep blue

Galtonia candicans

trumpets in spring. It needs well-drained soil
and protection from hot sun. H: 8cm (3in) S:
30cm (1ft). *G. asclepiadea* has long stems of
blue flowers in late summer. H: 75cm (30in)
S: 45cm (18in). *G. sino-ornata* is an acid-
loving, autumn-flowering species. H: 8cm
(3in) S: 30cm (1ft). *G ternifolia*, also acid-
loving, has pale blue flowers in autumn. H:
8cm (3in) S: 30cm (1ft). Hardiness 4 ☼ ☁

Geranium Hardy geraniums are tough,
reliable perennials that make good ground
cover in sun and shade with flowers in shades
of pink, blue, purple and white. They are
tolerant of most soils and flower in summer.
G. 'Ann Folkard' has trailing growths with
yellow leaves and magenta flowers. H: 60cm
(2ft) S: 1m (3ft). *G. cinereum* is a dwarf plant
with grey leaves; 'Ballerina' has pink flowers
and var. *subcaulescens* has magenta blooms.
H: 15cm (6in) S: 30cm (1ft). *G. endressii*
forms clumps of hairy leaves with pink
flowers. H: 45cm (18in) S: 60cm (2ft).
G. himalayense 'Plenum' has double, purple
flowers. H: 25cm (10in) S: 45cm (18in).
G. macrorrhizum has scented foliage and pink
flowers, 'Variegatum' has cream-edged leaves.
H: 30cm (1ft) S: 60cm (2ft). *G. x oxonianum*
'Wargrave Pink' is a spreading plant with pink
flowers. H: 60cm (2ft) S: 1m (3ft). *G. phaeum*
has dusky purple flowers. H: 80cm (32in) S:
45cm (18in). *G. pratense* has divided leaves
and blue flowers. H: 80cm (32in) S: 60cm
(2ft). *G. procurrens* has deep purple flowers.
H: 45cm (18in) S: 1m (3ft). *G. renardii* has
scalloped grey leaves and white flowers.
H: 30cm (1ft) S: 30cm (1ft). *G. traversii* has
grey leaves and pink flowers. H: 10cm (4in)
S: 30cm (1ft). Hardiness 4 ☼ ☁ ◊

Gladiolus 'The Bride' Most gladiolus are
stiffly upright cormous perennials but 'The
Bride' is a delicate, and tender, hybrid with
pure white flowers in early summer. H: 60cm
(2ft) S: 5cm (2in). Hardiness 2–3 ☼

Gleditsia triacanthos 'Sunburst' This small,
prickly tree is a good alternative to *Robinia
pseudoacacia* 'Frisia' where there is less
space and a brighter tree is required. The
foliage is yellow when young. The tree is
narrow at first, becoming conical with age.
H: 12m (40ft) S: 8m (25ft). Hardiness 4 ☼ ◊

Garrya elliptica

Gunnera magellanica

Globularia repens Globularias are mat-
forming evergreen shrubs for the rock garden
with true blue flowers in summer. They
require full sun and protection from excess
moisture in winter. *G. repens* is lower than
most. H: 5cm (2in) S: 15cm (6in).
Hardiness 4 ☼ ◊

Glyceria maxima var. *variegata* This rapidly
spreading grass has bright, white-striped
foliage. It is adaptable and will survive in
moist soil or in ponds in up to 75cm (30in) of
water. H: 80cm (32in) S: at least 1m (3ft).
Hardiness 4 ☼ ☁ ◖

Gunnera This genus ranges from tiny
creeping plants to huge rhizomatous
perennials with the largest leaves of any
frost-hardy plant. The best-known is
G. manicata which has leaves up to 2m (6ft)
high and across. *G. magellanica* is a slightly
tender perennial with scalloped dark green
leaves 8cm (3in) across and orange berries in
late summer. H: 15cm (6in) S: more than
30cm (1ft). Hardiness 3–4 ☼ ☁ ◖

Gymnocarpium dryopteris This vivid green,
deciduous, rhizomatous fern has triangular
fronds and spreads widely in acid or neutral,
moist, woodland soils in shade. H: 20cm (8in)
S: 1m (3ft). Hardiness 4 ☁ ◖

Gypsophila With their summer masses of
delicate five-petalled flowers in shades of
white and pink, these are plants for dry
alkaline soils. The taller cultivars are good for
cutting and the rock garden types can be
planted to tumble over walls. *G. aretioides* is a
compact, domed evergreen perennial with
dense foliage and white flowers. H: 5cm (2in)
S: 15cm (6in). *G. pacifica*, perennial, has large
pale pink flowers and tolerates moist soil.
H: 1m (3ft) S: 60cm (2ft). *G. repens* is a semi-
evergreen trailing perennial with pink flowers.
H: 20cm (8in) S: 50cm (20in).
G. 'Rosenschleir' is a semi-evergreen perennial
with a hazy dome of pale pink, double flowers.
H: 50cm (20in) S: 1m (3ft). Hardiness 4 ☼ ◊

Haberlea rhodopensis This exotic-looking
perennial, resembling an African violet, grows
best in rock crevices in moist, acid or neutral
soil in partial shade. Some protection from
winter wet is useful though plants will
tolerate low temperatures. H: 15cm (6in)
S: 25cm (10in). Hardiness 4 ☁ ☁

Hacquetia epipactis In late spring this
perennial forms a dome of bright lime-green
ruffs around a tuft of tiny, yellow flowers. It
is hardy but tends to prefer moist, humus-
rich soil and partial shade. H: 15cm (6in)
S: 15cm (6in).Hardiness 4 ☼ ☁

x *Halimocistus wintonensis* This evergreen shrub is a hybrid of *Halimium* and *Cistus*, both sun-loving plants that tolerate drought. It requires a well-drained soil and full sun and will then produce white flowers above the grey leaves in early summer. 'Merrist Wood Cream' has cream, dark-eyed flowers. H: 60cm (2ft) S: 1m (3ft). Hardiness 4 ☼ ◊

Hebe Hebes are good evergreens for coastal areas where the tender, large-leaved hybrids thrive. The cultivars and species vary and flowers can be white, pink or purple short spikes. *H.* 'Midsummer Beauty' has purple flowers in summer. H: 2m (6ft) S: 1.5m (5ft). *H.* 'Mrs Winder' has violet flowers in late summer. H: 1m (3ft) S: 1.2m (4ft). *H. odora* has white flowers in early summer. H: 1m (5ft) S: 1.5m (5ft). *H.* 'Pewter Dome' is low-growing with grey leaves and white flowers. H: 45cm (18in) S: 60cm (2ft). *H. pimeleoides* has grey leaves and white flowers. H: 45cm (18in) S: 60cm (2ft). *H.* 'Red Edge' has grey leaves, lined with red, and white flowers. H: 45cm (18in) S: 60cm (2ft). *H.* 'Rosie' has profuse pink flowers. H: 45cm (18in) S: 60cm (2ft). Hardiness 4 ☼ ◊ ✿ ⚕ - spring

Hedera Versatile evergreen plants that can be used as ground cover or as climbers, ivies root as they climb so need no support, and grow in dense shade. Their flowers are not showy but the variegated cultivars provide colour all year. *H. canariensis* 'Gloire de Marengo' is a large-leaved, slightly frost-tender ivy with grey-edged leaves, tinged pink in cold weather. H: 4m (13ft). *H. helix* has many variants and is fully hardy: 'Anne Marie' is edged with white. 'Buttercup' is bright yellow in sun. 'Eva' is edged white. 'Glacier' is white, grey and green. 'Goldheart' has small leaves with gold centres. 'Green Ripple' has deeply cut, deeply veined leaves. 'Hazel' has cream and green-speckled leaves. 'Manda's Crested' has star-shaped, green leaves. 'Sagittifolia Variegata' has narrow, white-edged leaves. H: 3m (10ft). *H. hibernica* is good for ground cover. H: 10cm (4in) S: 2m (6ft). Hardiness 4 ☼ ☁ ☁ ◊ ✿ ⚕

Helianthemum These are dwarf, evergreen shrubs with grey or green leaves and silky flowers in summer. They prefer dry, sunny

Hedera sagittifolia 'Variegata'

Helleborus lividus

positions and are ideal for large rock gardens or between paving. *H.* 'Beech Park Red' has bright red flowers. H: 20cm (8in) S: 60cm (2ft). *H. nummularium* has yellow flowers. H: 15cm (6in) S: 60cm (2ft). *H.* 'Rhodanthe Carneum' has grey leaves and pink flowers. H: 30cm (1ft) S: 60cm (2ft). Hardiness 4 ☼ ◊

Helichrysum This varied genus includes hardy perennials, annuals and shrubs, and their flowers are useful for cutting and drying. Most have hairy leaves and papery flowers and prefer dry soils and sun. *H. petiolare* is a tender, sprawling shrub with grey leaves. 'Limelight' has lime-green leaves. H: 50cm (20in) S: 2m (6ft). Hardiness 3 ☼ ◊ *H. splendidum* is a grey, evergreen shrub with gold, globular flowers in late summer. H: 1.2m (4ft) S: 1.2m (4ft). Hardiness 4 ☼ ◊

Helictotrichon sempervirens This evergreen grass forms a tuft of narrow grey-blue leaves and in midsummer produces stiff stems with small straw-coloured flowers. It thrives in alkaline, dry soils in sun. H: 1.5m (5ft) S: 60cm (2ft). Hardiness 4 ☼ ◊

Heliopsis helianthoides Heliopsis are useful perennials to bring bright gold and yellow to the late-summer garden. The tall, leafy stems support the large, daisy-like flowers. Well-

drained soil and full sun are preferred. *H. helianthoides* has many cultivars such as var. *scabra* 'Incomparabilis' with double flowers. H: 1.2m (4ft) S: 60cm (2ft). Hardiness 4 ☼ ✿

Helleborus Hellebores have two types of growth; most are herbaceous, forming dense tufts of leaves and flower stems arising directly from the soil, but some form woody, biennial shoots that flower in their second year and then die. They are hardy and valued for their winter and early-spring flowers. They need moist but well-drained soil and tolerate lime and some shade. *H. argutifolius* is shrubby with apple-green flowers. H: 1.2m (4ft) S: 1m (3ft). *H. foetidus* is shrubby with green and maroon flowers above finely cut leaves. H: 75cm (30in) S: 60cm (2ft). *H. lividus* is rather tender with shrubby growth and pinkish flowers. H: 45cm (18in) S: 30cm (1ft). *H. orientalis* is low-growing with pink, white, green or yellow flowers. H: 45cm (18in) S: 60cm (2ft). *H.* x *sternii* is a hybrid between *H. argutifolius* and *H. lividus*. H: 40cm (16in) S: 30cm (1ft). Hardiness 4 ☼ ☁ ☁

Hemerocallis The day lilies are clump-forming perennials with arching, grass-like foliage and thick fleshy roots. In summer the large, showy, trumpet-shaped flowers are produced over a long period. Each flower lasts just one day but each stem produces a succession of new blooms. Flower colour ranges from yellow, orange and red to pink but no pure white. *H.* 'Hyperion' has fragrant yellow flowers. H: 1m (3ft) S: 75cm (30in). *H.* 'Marion Vaughn' has large, scented, pale yellow flowers in late summer. H: 85cm (34in) S: 75cm (30in). Hardiness 4 ☼ ☁ ◓ ✾

Hesperis matronalis This biennial or short-lived perennial has rosettes of deep green, coarse leaves. In summer the tall, branched stems are covered with small, four-petalled flowers in shades of white and purple. These are sweetly scented. H: 1m (3ft) S: 45cm (18in). Hardiness 4 ☼ ☁ ✾

Heuchera These hardy herbaceous perennials have woody rootstocks and are grown for their leaves, which may be green or purple and often attractively marbled with silver, or for their sprays of small flowers. In moist soil they tolerate shade but the leaf colour may be less intense. *H. micrantha* var. *diversifolia* 'Palace Purple' has beetroot-red leaves and sprays of tiny, white flowers. H: 85cm (34in) S: 45cm (18in). Hardiness 4 ☼ ☁

Hibiscus This is a varied genus that includes frost-tender shrubs, hardy shrubs, herbaceous plants and annuals. The evergreens are not frost-hardy, unlike the deciduous *H. syriacus.* The herbaceous *H. moscheutos* has huge (20cm[8in]) pink or red flowers in summer It should be treated as a half-hardy annual in cold climates. H: 2m (6ft) S: 1m (3ft). *H. trionum* is a beautiful, erect annual with maroon-centred, cream flowers and inflated buds in summer. H: 75cm (30in) S: 45cm (18in). Hardiness 1–4 ☼

Hippophae rhamnoides This thorny, deciduous shrub has narrow, silver leaves. The small spring flowers are followed by orange berries on female plants. It is a tough plant that tolerates drought and is a useful wind-break in coastal gardens. H: 6m (20ft) S: 6m (20ft). Hardiness 4 ☼ ◊

Hosta These hardy, herbaceous perennials are grown for their bold foliage which can be used as ground cover. Hundreds of cultivars offer a variety of foliage colours and shapes. The tubular summer flowers in lilac or white are good for cutting. Hostas tolerate most soils but slugs and snails attack the leaves. *H.* 'Aureomarginata' has leaves edged in yellow. H: 75cm (30in) S: 1m (3ft). *H.* 'Bressingham Blue' has blue-grey leaves. H: 60cm (2ft) S: 75cm (30in). *H. fortunei* var. *aureomarginata* has yellow-edged leaves and mauve flowers. H: 60cm (2ft) S: 75cm (30in). *H.* (Tardiana Group) 'Halcyon' has blue leaves and greyish flowers. H: 40cm (16in) S: 75cm (30in). *H. lancifolia* has narrow, glossy leaves. H: 45cm (18in) S: 75cm (30in). *H. rohdeifolia* f. *albopicta* has narrow leaves edged with yellow, and purple flowers. H: 30cm (1ft) S: 45cm (18in). *H. sieboldiana* var. *elegans* has blue-grey leaves and lilac flowers. H: 1m (3ft) S: 1.2m (4ft). *H. undulata* var. *univittata* has leaves with a bold central white splash. H: 45cm (18in) S: 75cm (30in). Hardiness 4 ☼ ☁

Houttuynia cordata This creeping herbaceous perennial has heart-shaped leaves that smell of citrus when crushed. The white flowers are produced throughout summer. It can be planted as a marginal plant in ponds. 'Chameleon' has bold variegated foliage of red, yellow and green. 'Flame' is even brighter. H: 30cm (1ft) S: 75cm (30in). Hardiness 4 ☼ ☁ ◓ ✾

Houttuynia cordata 'Chameleon'

Humulus lupulus 'Aureus' The yellow-leaved form of the hop is a vigorous, twining, herbaceous climber. In late summer the stems are covered in 'hops' which can be dried for display. The leaves are brightest when grown in full sun, but can scorch in dry soil. H: 6m (20ft). Hardiness 4 ☼ ☁ ◓

Hyacinthoides non-scripta The English bluebell has narrower, deeper bells than the Spanish bluebell (*Hyacinthoides hispanica*). In late spring it creates a carpet of flowers in deciduous woodland and spreads by self-sown seed. The sap may cause skin irritation. H: 45cm (18in) S: 8cm (3in). Hardiness 4 ☼ ☁

Hydrangea anomala subsp. *petiolaris* Most hydrangeas are deciduous, free-standing shrubs, but *H. anomala* subsp. *petiolaris* is a self-clinging climber that thrives in shade. The clusters of white flowers are produced in early summer. H: 15m (50ft). Hardiness 4 ☼ ☁ ☁ ✄ after flowering.

Hyoscyamus niger This annual has sticky leaves with an unpleasant smell, and arching stems with pale, buff flowers veined with purple. They are followed by attractive 'shuttlecock' seed pods. It thrives in poor soil and self-seeds. All parts are toxic. H: 60cm (2ft) S: 60cm (2ft). Hardiness 4 ☼ ◊

Hypericum These hardy shrubs have showy, bright yellow flowers with prominent stamens in summer. They vary from dwarf ground cover and shrubs to hedging plants. Some vaiegated plants are grown for their foliage, and others have attractive seedheads. *H. androsaemum* has small flowers and black fruit. H: 75cm (30in) S: 1m (3ft). *H.* 'Hidcote' is evergreen with golden flowers. H: 1.2m (4ft) S: 1.5m (5ft). *H. perforatum* is a perennial for the wild garden. H: 1m (3ft) S: 60cm (2ft). Hardiness 4 ☼ ◊ ✽ ✄

Iberis sempervirens This dwarf, evergreen shrub has dark green, tiny leaves and clusters of bright, white flowers in spring. It is useful in the rock garden. H: 30cm (1ft) S: 40cm (16in). 'Weisser Zwerg' is more compact. H: 15cm (6in) S: 25cm (10in). Hardiness 4 ☼ ◊ ◓ ✽ ✄ – after flowering

Ilex aquifolium The evergreen common holly can be grown as a specimen shrub or as hedging. The variegated cultivars bring colour to the garden in winter and female plants have red or yellow berries in winter. They withstand clipping and pruning to control their size. 'J. C. van Tol' is a self-fertile female with good, red berries. H: 6m (20ft) S: 3cm (10ft). Hardiness 4 ☀ ☁ ◕ ✻

Iris There is an iris for every situation, from the pond to the rock garden. Most are hardy perennials grown for their flowers, though some have variegated foliage. Bearded irises prefer sun and well-drained soil. *I.* 'Blue Shimmer' has blue and white flowers. H: 75cm (30in) S: 30cm (1ft). *I.* 'Cherry Garden' is mauve. H: 25cm (10in) S: 30cm (1ft). *I.* 'Florentina' has fragrant, white flowers. H: 75cm (30in) S: 30cm (1ft). *I.* 'Green Spot' is ivory with green markings. H: 25cm (10in) S: 30cm (1ft). *I. pallida* has fragrant pale blue flowers and 'Variegata' has yellow-striped leaves. H: 1m (3ft) S: 30cm (1ft). *I. pumila* is a dwarf species with yellow or purple flowers. H: 15cm (6in) S: 30cm (1ft). There are other types of iris for gardens. *I. cristata* has lavender blue flowers and prefers moist, acid soil. H: 10cm (4in) S: 15cm (6in). *I. danfordiae* is a dwarf bulbous species with

Ilex aquifolium 'J. C. van Tol'

bright yellow flowers in early spring. H: 15cm (5in). *I. foetidissima* has evergreen leaves, dull-purple flowers and bright orange seeds. *I. foetidissima* var. *citrina* has yellow flowers and 'Variegata' has white-striped leaves but no flowers. H: 60cm (2ft) S: 60cm (2ft). *I. laevigata* is a water iris with blue flowers. H: 75cm (30in) S: 60cm (2ft). *I. pseudacorus* is a water iris with yellow flowers and 'Variegata' has yellow-striped leaves in spring. H: 1m (3ft) S: 1m (3ft). *I. sanguinea* has purple flowers in moist soil. H: 75cm (30in) S: 60cm (2ft). *I. sibirica* has blue flowers in moist soil. H: 75cm (30in) S: 60cm (2ft). *I. spuria* is a tall species with many cultivars. H: 1m (3ft) S: 60cm (2ft). *I. unguicularis* is a winter-flowering species for hot, dry soil. H: 30cm (1ft) S: 30cm (1ft). *I. versicolor* is an iris for moist soil with purple flowers. H: 75cm (30in) S: 45cm (18in). Hardiness 4 ☀ ☁ ◔ ◕

Itea ilicifolia This evergreen shrub can be grown against a wall to protect it from strong wind and cold. It is a large shrub with glossy, holly-like leaves and pendulous spikes of tiny green vanilla-scented flowers in late summer. It will grow in most soils. H: 3m (10ft) S: 3m (10ft). Hardiness 3–4 ☀ ☁ ✾ ✻ - spring

Jasminum The summer-flowering, scented jasmine is a vigorous twiner. *J. officinale* 'Argentovariegatum' has white flowers and cream-edged leaves. H: 12m (40ft). Hardiness 4 ☀ ◔ ✾ ✻ - spring. *J. nudiflorum* is a straggly shrub with yellow, starry, scentless flowers in winter. Cut out the old stems to encourage new green shoots that will flower freely. H: 3m (10ft) S: 3m (10ft). Hardiness 4 ☀ ☁ ◔ ◕ ✻ - after flowering

Jeffersonia dubia This deciduous, woodland perennial has large rounded leaves and delicate, cup-shaped, lilac flowers in early summer. It needs moist, humus-rich soil. H: 20cm (8in) S: 30cm (1ft). Hardiness 4 ☁ ☁

Juncus effusus This common rush will grow in water logged, acid soil and bogs. The cultivar 'Spiralis' is a popular pond plant with curious, spirally curled stems that form a low, twisted clump that is green all year. It has no beauty in flower. H: 45cm (18in) S: 60cm (2ft). Hardiness 4 ☀ ☁ ◕

Juniperus Junipers are prickly conifers with fine foliage that tolerate drought and cold better than other sorts. The gold and blue-grey cultivars provide winter colour. They withstand regular clipping. *J. communis* is the source of juniper berries. H: 5m (16ft) S: 3m (10ft). 'Compressa' is dwarf and narrow. H: 75cm (30in) S: 45cm (18in). *J. squamata* 'Blue Carpet' has blue-grey, prickly foliage on squat plants. H: 30cm (1ft) S: 1m (3ft). *J.* x *pfitzeriana* Gold Sovereign has yellow foliage. H: 1m (3ft) S: 1m (3ft). Hardiness 4 ☀ ☁ ◔ ✻ - summer

Kale 'Russian Red' This hardy vegetable is grown for its young shoots which are tasty and nutritious. It thrives in alkaline clay and this cultivar has wavy-edged, red foliage.

Knautia arvensis This perennial has large quantities of small, rounded, lilac flower-heads in late summer. It thrives in alkaline soil. H: 1.2m (4ft) S: 30cm (1ft). Hardiness 4 ☀ ◔ ✾

Kniphofia Red hot pokers are striking perennials that make strong clumps of narrow leaves and produce thick stems with oval heads of tubular flowers in orange and yellow. They require moist, but well-drained, fertile soil. *K.* 'Ice Queen' has pale cream flowers. H: 1.5m (5ft) S: 75cm (30in). *K.* 'Little Maid' has narrow spikes of cream flowers. H: 60cm (2ft) S: 45cm (18in). Hardiness 4 ☀ ◕

Kolkwitzia amabilis Called the beauty bush because of its pretty, pink, tubular flowers in early summer, it rapidly becomes a rounded, deciduous shrub, and can be planted as a specimen or hedge. 'Pink Cloud' has brighter flowers without the yellow throat of the ordinary species. H: 3m (10ft) S: 4m (10ft). Hardiness 4 ☀ ◔

Lamium The lamiums are deadnettles and quickly grow into perennial weed-smothering clumps of ground cover with attractive foliage and small flowers in summer. They thrive in moist soil but will also tolerate shade and drier soil. *L. album* is the white deadnettle with plain green leaves. H: 30cm (1ft) S: 60cm (2ft). *L. galeobdolon* has silver-splashed leaves and yellow flowers, and can be

Iris siberica 'Perry's Blue'

Lathyrus grandiflorus

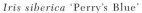

invasive. H: 30cm (3ft) S: 1m (3ft). *L. maculatum* has purple flowers and the cultivars show great variation. 'White Nancy' has silver leaves and white flowers and 'Beacon Silver' has purple flowers. H: 15cm (6in) S: 60cm (2ft). Hardiness 4 ☼ ☁ ☁ ✿

Lathyrus These annuals and perennials have pea-shaped flowers in summer and grow well in fertile soil. *L. grandiflorus* is a slender herbaceous climber with crimson, scentless flowers. H: 1.5m (5ft). *L. latifolius* is the everlasting sweet pea, a herbaceous climber with scentless flowers. *L. odoratus* is the annual sweet pea with many cultivars. H: 2.5m (8ft). *L. rotundifolius* is a herbaceous climber with clusters of small purple-red flowers. H: 1m (3ft). Hardiness 4 ☼ ☁ ◊

Laurus nobilis Bay is an evergreen shrub that is hardy but may be damaged by severe frost. It withstands pruning and is easily trained into standards and other ornamental shapes. It can be grown in pots and will withstand hot, dry conditions. The small flowers have no ornamental value. H: 10m (33ft) S: 8m (25ft). Hardiness 4 ☼ ☁ ◊ ◊ ⚔

Lavandula Lavenders are small, evergreen shrubs with fragrant foliage that is usually grey. The spikes of fragrant, small flowers are

usually purple or white, The many hybrids are grown more often than the species. They can be used as low hedges. *L. angustifolia* has deep purple flowers in summer, H: 1m (3ft) S: 1.2m (4ft). 'Munstead' is more compact. H: 45cm (18in) S: 60cm (2ft). *L. x intermedia* is a large lavender and 'Hidcote Giant' has purple flowers. H: 1m (3ft) S: 1.2m (4ft). *L. lanata* has white, woolly leaves and dark purple flowers, and needs dry soil. H: 60cm (2ft) S: 1m (3ft). *L. stoechas* has grey leaves and short purple bracts on the flowerheads. The subspecies *pedunculata* has longer flower stems. H: 60cm (2ft) S: 60cm (2ft). Hardiness 4 ☼ ◊ ◊ ✿ ⚔

Lavatera 'Barnsley' The shrubby, hardy lavateras are short-lived, fast-growing shrubs with masses of pink flowers through summer. They have greyish leaves. In rich soil they grow too fast and tend to break. 'Barnsley' has white, pink-eyed flowers. H: 2m (6ft) S: 2m (6ft). Hardiness 4 ☼ ◊ ⚔ - spring

Leontopodium alpinum This perennial alpine has star-shaped flowerheads made from insignificant flowers and long, woolly bracts. It requires gritty, alkaline or neutral soil and full sun. It needs protection from winter wet. 'Mignon' is a smaller cultivar. H: 10cm (4in) S: 10cm (4in). Hardiness 4 ☼ ◊

Lettuce As well as being fast-growing salad crops, the wide variety of leaf types and colours makes lettuce suitable for edging vegetable plots and potagers. 'Lollo Rosso' is especially attractive.

Lewisia cotyledon These succulent alpine perennials flower in early summer in a variety of colours from white, through yellow and orange to deep pink and purple. The evergreen rosettes are prone to rot in winter and should be planted in vertical crevices in the rock garden. They require perfect drainage. H: 25cm (10in) S: 25cm (10in). Hardiness 4 ☼ ◊

Liatris spicata This tough herbaceous perennial has narrow, grassy leaves and stiff stems of fluffy, purple flowers in late summer. They will grow in most soils and are good for cutting. H: 1.5m (5ft) S: 45cm (18in). 'Kobold' is a shorter cultivar. H: 45cm (18in) S: 45cm (18in). Hardiness 4 ☼ ☁ ✿

Libertia formosa This rhizomatous perennial forms clumps of narrow, upright leaves that are deep green all year. In early summer they produce wiry stems with masses of small, three-petalled, white flowers. It prefers moist, well-drained soil and a sheltered spot. H: 1m (3ft) S: 60cm (2ft). Hardiness 4 ☼ ☁

Ligustrum ovalifolium The common, evegreen hedging privet tolerates moist soils and conditions, growing best in sun and rich soil. The colourful golden leaves of the cultivar 'Aureum' have a bright yellow margin. The small white flowers are of no beauty. H: 3m (10ft) S: 2m (6ft). Hardiness 4 ☼ ☁ ◊ ⚔ - spring or summer

Lilium Some of these bulbous perennials are difficult to grow. Modern hybrids are easy but most are prone to slug damage and virus diseases spread by aphids. Most like moist soil and flower in summer. *L. auratum* has huge, white, scented flowers. It is more difficult than similar Oriental hybrids. H: 1.5m (5ft) S: 25cm (10in). *L. candidum* has white scented flowers and must be planted on the surface. H: 1.5m (5ft) S: 25cm (10in). *L. formosanum* var. *pricei* is dwarf with up to three white, scented flowers. H: 25cm (10in) S: 15cm (6in). *L.* 'Green Magic'. has scented,

white, green-flushed flowers. H: 2m (6ft)
S: 25cm (10in). *L. lancifolium* is the tiger lily
with orange, spotted flowers. H: 1.5m (5ft)
S: 25cm (10in). *L. martagon* has small, pink
flowers. H: 2m (6ft) S: 25cm (10in).
L. martagon var. *album* has white flowers.
H: 2m (6ft) S: 25cm (10in). *L. regale* is
robust with white, scented flowers. H: 1.5m
(5ft) S: 25cm (10in). Hardiness 4 ☼ ⛅ ⊛

Limonium platyphyllum This is a perennial
sea lavender with clumps of broad, glossy,
deep green leaves. In late summer these are
smothered by a domed cloud of tiny lavender
flowers on wiry stems. H: 60cm (2ft) S: 1m
(3ft). Hardiness 4 ☼ ◊ ✿

Linaria The toadflaxes have narrow leaves on
bushy plants and small 'snapdragon' flowers
in a range of colours in summer. Most prefer
sun and well-drained soil. *L. purpurea* is a
tall perennial with small, purple flowers.
'Canon Went' has bright pink flowers. H: 1m
(3ft) S: 25cm (10in). *L. vulgaris* is a creeping
perennial with soft yellow flowers. H: 60cm
(2ft) S: 30cm (1ft). Hardiness 4 ☼ ◊

Linnaea borealis This slender, creeping,
evergreen shrub thrives only in humus-rich,
moist, acid soil and will not tolerate drought.
In summer it produces pairs of small, pink,
bell-shaped flowers on short, thin stems. H:
8cm (4in) S: 1m (3ft). Hardiness 4 ⛅

Linum This genus includes the common flax,
hardy annuals and dwarf shrubs. The shrubs
and perennials prefer sunny, dry sites and
have white, yellow or sky blue flowers on thin,
upright, stems. *L.* 'Gemmel's Hybrid' is
evergreen with large, yellow flowers in
summer. H: 15cm (6in) S: 20cm (8in).
L. perenne is a perennial with narrow, blue-
green leaves and pale blue flowers in
summer. H: 60cm (2ft) S: 25cm (10in).
Hardiness 4 ☼ ◊ ✿

Lobelia Lobelias include the common
bedding plant and spectacular herbaceous
perennials with erect spikes of flowers in
summer. The perennials prefer moist soil and
are popular plants for pond margins.
L. erinus, the bedding lobelia, has thin stems
and small flowers. H: 15cm (6in) S: 25cm

Lonicera japonica 'Halliana'

(10in). *L.* 'Brightness' is a hardy perennial
with pink flowers. H: 75cm (30in) S: 25cm
(10in). *L. cardinalis* has red-tinted, bright
green leaves and scarlet flowers. H: 75cm
(30in) S: 25cm (10in). *L.* 'Dark Crusader' has
maroon stems and red flowers. H: 75cm
(30in) S: 25cm (10in). *L.* 'Queen Victoria' has
maroon leaves and scarlet flowers. H: 75cm
(30in) S: 25cm (10in). Hardiness 4 ☼ ◖

Lonicera The honeysuckles are best-known
for the climbing species, many of which have
fragrant blooms, but there are also evergreen
and deciduous shrubs suitable for hedging
and as specimen plants. *L. japonica* 'Halliana'
is a strong twiner with white, scented flowers
through summer that age to cream.
H: 10m (33ft). *L. nitida* 'Baggesen's Gold' is a
small-leaved evergreen shrub with gold
leaves. H: 1.5m (5ft) S: 1.5m (5ft). *L.
periclymenum* is a deciduous twiner with
fragrant flowers in summer. H: 7m (22ft). *L.
pileata* is a spreading evergreen shrub with
small leaves. H: 75cm (30in) S: 2.5m (8ft).
Hardiness 4 ☼ ⛅ ⛅ ⊛ ✿ ✂ –
summer or after flowering

Lunaria The biennial *L. annua* is grown for
its purple or white flowers in late spring and
the translucent seedheads later in the year. It
self-seeds in many gardens. H: 75cm (30in)

Lysichiton americanus

S: 30cm (1ft). *L. rediviva* is perennial with
lilac, scented flowers and narrow pods. H: 1m
(3ft) S: 30cm (1ft). Hardiness 4 ☼ ⛅ ◗ ⊛

Lupinus arboreus This short-lived evergreen
shrub grows quickly from seed. In coastal
gardens it withstands salt spray but it may be
damaged in cold, inland gardens. The spikes
of creamy-yellow flowers are produced in
early summer. H: 1.5m (5ft) S:2m (6ft).
Hardiness 4 ☼ ◊ ✿

Lychnis These are biennials and perennials,
often with grey or purple leaves and clusters
of five-petalled flowers in shades of pink,
magenta and scarlet. They vary from delicate
perennials to good border plants in strident
colours. *L. chalcedonica* has bright green
leaves and upright stems with tight clusters
of small scarlet flowers in summer. H: 1.2m
(4ft) S: 30cm (1ft). *L. flos-cuculi* is the
ragged robin with deeply cut, pale pink petals
in late spring. It prefers moist soil. H: 75cm
(30in) S: 60cm (2ft). Hardiness 4 ☼ ⛅

Lycium barbarum This sprawling, deciduous
shrub survives coastal winds and makes a
good windbreak. The grey leaves are dotted
with small purple flowers in summer, and
orange berries in autumn. H: 2m (6ft) S:
2.5m (8ft). Hardiness 4 ☼ ◊ ✂ spring

Lysichiton americanus The skunk cabbage, a marginal perennial, forms huge clumps of glossy, coarse leaves in summer but in spring it brightens large ponds or bog gardens with huge, yellow 'arum' flowers. It grows in moist soil or shallow water. H: 1m (3ft) S: 1.2m (4ft). Hardiness 4 ☼ ☁ 💧

Lysimachia nummularia 'Aurea' This creeping, evergreen perennial forms a mat of small rounded, golden leaves, studded in summer with yellow flowers. It thrives in moist soil and even grows over waterfalls. Its trailing growth is useful in hanging baskets. H: 5cm (2in) S: 1m (3ft). Hardiness 4 ☼ ☁ 💧

Lythrum These perennials have square stems and terminal spikes of small, starry flowers. Most prefer moist soil. *L. salicaria* has tall spikes of pink or mauve flowers in late summer. Cultivars have brighter flowers and more compact habit. H: 1.2m (4ft) S: 45cm (18in). *L. virgatum* 'The Rocket' has narrow spikes of purple-red flowers. H: 75cm (30in) S: 45cm (18in). Hardiness 4 ☼ ☁

Macleaya cordata This is the plume poppy, grown for its large heads of bronze and cream feathery flowerheads in summer and large, scalloped leaves that are grey, and white beneath. This is a strong-growing, suckering perennial for large borders. H: 2.5m (8ft) S: 1m (3ft). Hardiness 4 ☼ ☁

Mahonia pinnata (M. x *wagneri* 'Pinnacle') Mahonias are evergreen shrubs with glossy leaves, divided into prickly leaflets, and clusters or spikes of yellow flowers in winter or early spring. These are often scented and followed by black berries. Most prefer some shade but will grow in sun if the soil is not too dry. *M. pinnata* has wavy-edged leaves that turn red in winter, and yellow flowers in spring. H: 2m (6ft) S: 2m (6ft). Hardiness 4 ☼ ☁ ☁ ✿ ✂ - spring

Malva moschata This herbaceous perennial is called musk mallow, but the flowers are scentless, and only the leaves have a faint, musky scent. The flowers in summer are pale pink against the finely cut leaves. The white *M. moschata* f. *alba* is especially attractive. H: 1m (3ft) S: 60cm (2ft). Hardiness 4 ☼ ☁

Matteuccia struthiopteris This rhizomatous, hardy, deciduous fern produces 'shuttlecocks' of fronds. These are especially attractive in spring when they first emerge a bright, pale green. It will spread into clumps of separate 'shuttlecocks' and thrives in moist, woodland soil. H: 1m (3ft) S: 1m (3ft). Hardiness 4 ☁ ☁

Matthiola incana Stocks are usually treated as biennials although the single, wild form is sometimes grown as a short-lived, dwarf shrub in light, dry soil. The grey leaves augment the fragrant flowers that open in late spring. It prefers alkaline soil and is prone to clubroot disease. Modern hybrids have a range of habits, and flowers in shades of pink, white and purple. H: 60cm (2ft) S: 60cm (2ft). Hardiness 4 ☼ 💧 ✿

Meconopsis cambrica The perennial Welsh poppy is a robust plant that self-seeds profusely and bears yellow or orange flowers from spring to autumn. *M. cambrica flore-pleno* has double flowers. 'Frances Perry' has red flowers. H: 45cm (18in) S: 25cm (10in). Hardiness 4 ☼ ☁ ☁ 💧

Melianthus major This bold foliage plant is hardy in mild areas or sheltered places, but in cold areas it will be cut to ground level and will not produce its purple flowers from late spring. The stems of large leaves are deeply divided and blue-grey. H: 2m (6ft) S: 2m (6ft). Hardiness 3–4 ☼

Mentha Mints are mostly hardy, herbaceous, perennials with fragrant foliage and pale mauve flowers. Some should be restricted by planting in bottomless pots, sunk into the soil. They grow best in moist, rich soil. *M. aquatica* is water mint – a useful pond plant. H: 60cm (28ft) S: 1m (3ft).
M. pulegium is pennyroyal, a low, creeping, plant with pungent leaves. H: 25cm (10in) S: 1m (3ft). *M. suaveolens* is apple mint, with hairy, grey leaves and mauve flowers. H: 1m (3ft) S: 1m (3ft). 'Variegata' has white-edged leaves and a more compact habit. Hardiness 4 ☼ ☁ 💧 ✿ ❀

Menyanthes trifoliata The common bogbean is a marginal aquatic plant that sends thick shoots across the water surface, with tough leaves that look like broad bean foliage. The spikes of white, starry flowers are produced in summer. It is a useful plant to shade water but is too vigorous for small ponds. H: 20cm (8in) S: 1m (3ft). Hardiness 4 ☼

Mertensia pulmonarioides This pretty, blue-flowered herbaceous perennial forms strong clumps in moist soil in partial shade. The leaves are blue-green and the spring flowers are carried on upright stems. H: 45cm (18in) S: 25cm (10in). Hardiness 4 ☁ ☁

Mimulus cardinalis This genus contains the bedding plants that thrive in moist, shaded spots in the garden, and *M. guttatus* that thrives beside ponds. *M. cardinalis* is a tall perennial with hairy stems and leaves and a long succession of scarlet flowers in summer. H: 1m (3ft) S: 60cm (2ft). Hardiness 4 ☼ 💧

Miscanthus sinensis This is a deciduous grass with erect stems, narrow leaves and plumes of feathery pink or beige flowers in late summer. They prefer moist soil but will not tolerate waterlogged conditions in winter. *M. sinensis* var. *purpurascens* has purple-tinted leaves that turn orange in autumn. H: 1.2m (4ft) S: 1m (3ft). Hardiness 4 ☼ ☁

Matteuccia struthiopteris

Monarda didyma This hardy herbaceous perennial thrives in moist soil, spreading into large clumps. It has scented leaves and whorls of narrow flowers in summer that are commonly red or pink, but hybrids may also be mauve, lavender or white. In dry soil plants are prone to mildew. H: 1m (3ft) S: 60cm (2ft). Hardiness 4 ☼ ⛅ ⬤ 🌾 ✿

Morisia monanthos This small alpine perennial has deep green leaves in rosettes and bright gold flowers in spring and early summer. It requires perfect drainage and is best grown in troughs or raised beds. H: 5cm (2in) S: 10cm (4in). Hardiness 4 ☼ ◊

Muscari Grape hyacinths are dwarf, bulbous plants with grassy leaves and spikes of blue or white flowers in spring. The common *M. armeniacum* can seed in gardens and become a nuisance, but the double 'Blue Spike' does not spread. *M. latifolium* has broad leaves and deep blue and purple flowers. H: 15cm (6in) S: 5cm (2in). Hardiness 4 ☼ ⛅ ◊

Myosotis Forget-me-nots are biennial or perennial herbaceous plants with hairy leaves and blue flowers that often open pink and change colour. They are used beside ponds in moist soil or as spring bedding where they often self-seed. *M. scorpioides* is a perennial water plant with pale blue flowers. H: 30cm (1ft) S: 30cm (1ft). *M. sylvatica* is biennial and has been bred to produce a large number of cultivars such as 'Royal Blue'. H: 20cm (8in) S: 20cm (8in). Hardiness 4 ☼ ⛅ ⬤

Myriophyllum aquaticum This fast-growing, aquatic perennial has no floral beauty but the stems of feathery foliage are attractive. It will grow in water or in wet soil and is a useful oxygenator and sanctuary for pond life. In cold regions, pieces should be protected in a frost-free place for replanting in spring. H: 15cm (6in) S: 1m (3ft). Hardiness 3–4 ☼ ⛅

Myrtus communis This evergreen shrub has scented foliage and small, fluffy, white, fragrant flowers in late summer. It is slightly tender and can be grown in large pots in cold areas. It requires well-drained soil and a sunny position. H: 2.5m (8ft) S: 2.5m (8ft). Hardiness 3–4 ☼ ◊ 🌾 ⚔ – spring

Narcissus There is huge variation among narcissi, commonly called daffodils, but most are hardy and flower in spring in shades of yellow, white and orange. The dwarf species and cultivars are useful on rock gardens and for naturalizing in grass. They prefer moist soil and the foliage should be left to grow for six weeks after flowering before it is cut down. *N. bulbocodium* is the yellow, hoop petticoat daffodil with wide, flaring trumpets. H: 15cm (6in) S: 5cm (2in). *N. cyclamineus* is yellow with long, narrow trumpets and reflexed petals. H: 20cm (8in) S: 5cm (2in). *N.* 'February Gold' is an early yellow. H: 30cm (1ft) S: 10cm (4in). *N.* 'Tête-à-tête' has two yellow flowers per stem. H: 15cm (6in) S: 8cm (3in). *N.* 'Thalia' has clusters of pendent, white flowers. H: 35cm (14in) S: 10cm (4in). Hardiness 4 ☼ ⛅ 🌾

Nepeta Catmints have greyish, fragrant leaves and blue or yellow flowers. They sprawl over edges and make good edging, and ideal ground cover under roses. They are hardy, herbaceous perennials that flower in summer and thrive in sun. *N. govaniana* is upright with pale yellow flowers. H: 1m (6ft) S: 60cm (2ft). *N. nervosa* is bushy with purple-blue flowers. H: 60cm (2ft) S: 30cm (1ft). *N. racemosa* is spreading with lilac-blue flowers. H: 30cm (1ft) S: 45cm (18in).

Nymphaea 'Froebelii'

N. sibirica has grey leaves and lavender-blue flowers. H: 75cm (30in) S: 45cm (18in). *N.* 'Six Hills Giant' is vigorous with lavender-blue flowers. H: 75cm (30in) S: 60cm (2ft). Hardiness 4 ☼ ◊ 🌾 ✿

Nerine These slightly tender bulbs need sun and summer heat to flourish. They flower in autumn with bare stems of pink, starry flowers that are good for cutting. The bulbs and young foliage should be protected from frost. *N. bowdenii* is most hardy, with large pink flowers. H: 45cm (18in) S: 8cm (3in). *N. undulata* has pink, crinkled petals. H: 45cm (18in) S: 8cm (3in). Hardiness 3–4 ☼ ◊

Nicotiana Some nicotiana are perennial shrubs, but most are treated as half-hardy annuals for summer bedding. The annual *N. langsdorffii* has tubular, green flowers. H: 1.5m (5ft) S: 35cm (14n). *N.* 'Lime Green' has showy, pale green, large flowers. H: 60cm (2ft) S: 25cm (10in). *N. sylvestris* has tubular, white, scented flowers. H: 1.5m (5ft) S: 60cm (2ft). Hardiness 3 ☼ 🌾

Nymphaea Waterlilies are one of the few hardy perennials with large flowers that will grow in deep water in ponds. Their floating leaves shade water and prevent algal growth in ponds. They flower in summer, require sun and dislike running water. Blue-flowered cultivars are frost-tender. *N.* 'Amabilis' has pink flowers. S: 2m (6ft). *N.* 'Escarboucle' has red flowers and bronze-tinted leaves. S:1.5m (5ft). *N.* 'Firecrest' has pink flowers. S:1.2m (4ft). *N.* 'Froebelii' has red flowers. S:1m (3ft). *N.* 'Pink Sensation' has pink flowers and purple young leaves. S:1.2m (4ft). *N.* 'Pygmaea Helvola' has purple-mottled leaves and yellow flowers. S: 40cm (16in). Hardiness 4 ☼ 🌾

Nymphoides peltata This rapidly spreading aquatic perennial will grow in up to 60cm (2ft) of water. In summer its yellow, star-shaped flowers are produced just above the water. S: 2m (6ft). Hardiness 4 ☼

Oemleria cerasiformis This deciduous shrub is useful in wild areas or at the back of borders. It has hanging clusters of scented, white flowers in early spring and purple berries in late summer, and green leaves that turn yellow in autumn. They thrive and sucker in moist soil. H: 2.5m (8ft) S: 4m (13ft). Hardiness 4 ☼ ☁ ◗ ⦵ ⅄ after flowering

Olearia phlogopappa The daisy bushes are slightly tender evergreen shrubs that grow quickly but can be short-lived. Their flowers, in shades of white, pink and purple, often cover the branches in their profusion. *O. phlogopappa* has deep green leaves, white below, and white, blue or mauve flowers in early summer. H: 2m (6ft) S: 2m (6ft). Hardiness 3-4 ☼ ◌ ✿ ⅄ - after flowering

Olsynium douglasii Formerly known as a *Sisyrinchium*, this grassy-leaved herbaceous perennial prefers moist, well-drained soil and part shade. In summer it produces nodding, bell-shaped, purple flowers on thin stems. H: 30cm (1ft) S: 15cm (6in). Hardiness 4 ☼ ☁

Onopordum acanthium This is a robust, spiny biennial that thrives in sun in dry soil. In its first year it forms a large rosette of silver, prickly leaves and in the second it produces a tall, branched flower stem with purple, thistle flowers in summer. It may need staking in exposed gardens. H: 3m (10ft) S: 1m (3ft). Hardiness 4 ☼ ◌ ✿

Ophiopogon planiscapus 'Nigrescens' The value of this grass-like plant is the glossy, deep purple, almost black foliage. It forms tufts of leaves and spreads by underground shoots. In summer it produces short stems of lilac flowers, followed by black berries. It is best in acid, moist but well-drained soil. H: 20cm (8in) S: 30cm (1ft). Hardiness 4 ☼

Origanum These are mostly dwarf shrubs or herbaceous perennials that thrive in dry, alkaline soils. They have aromatic foliage and *O. vulgare* is the herb oregano. In summer they have clusters of small pink flowers and some have conspicuous pink bracts. They are useful for border edges and gravel gardens. *O.* 'Kent Beauty' is dwarf with green leaves and pink bracts. H: 10cm (4in) S: 20cm (8in). *O. laevigatum* has dark green leaves and pink flowers. H: 45cm (18in) S: 45cm (18in). *O. rotundifolium* has pink flowers in greenish bracts. H: 25cm (10in) S: 30cm (1ft).

Orontium aquaticum

Papaver orientale 'Patty's Plum'

O. vulgare has green leaves and pale pink flowers; 'Aureum' has yellow leaves. H: 60cm (2ft) S: 60cm (2ft). Hardiness 4 ☼ ◌ ⦵ ✿

Orontium aquaticum This submerged aquatic has blue-green leaves above the surface and curious yellow and white, thin flower spikes. It will grow in up to 45cm (18in) of water and will also grow in moist soil at the pond edge. H: 15cm (6in) S: 60cm (2ft). Hardiness 4 ☼

Osmanthus These evergreen shrubs have small, scented flowers. Some are very useful for hedges and topiary because they withstand regular clipping. They will grow in most soils and in shade though variegated cultivars tend to colour better in sun. *O. decorus* has oval leaves, white flowers in spring and black berries. H: 3m (10ft) S: 4m (13ft). *O. heterophyllus* has holly-like leaves and snow white flowers in late summer. H: 5m (16ft) S: 5m (16ft). Hardiness 4 ☼ ☁ ⦵ ⅄ - after flowering

Osmunda regalis This moisture-loving, deciduous fern does best at the pondside where it forms large mounds of blue-green fronds. The fertile fronds are produced in summer. It requires moist, humus-rich, acid soil but will grow in sun if the soil is moist. H: 2m (6ft) S: 1.2m (4ft). Hardiness 4 ☼ ☁

Osteospermum jucundum Osteospermums are slightly frost tender, evergreen shrubs or annuals with daisy-like flowers in summer. To stand the best chance of surviving winters they should be grown in full sun in dry soil. *O. jucundum* is low-growing and hardier than most, forming mats of foliage and producing its mauve flowers all summer. H: 30cm (1ft) S: 1m (3ft). Hardiness 3–4 ☼ ◌

Oxalis Some oxalis are considered weeds, but others are desirable garden plants. All have clover-like foliage and funnel-shaped flowers. *O. adenophylla* is bulbous with finely divided grey leaves and large pink and white flowers in spring. H: 10cm (4in) S: 15cm (6in). *O.* 'Ione Hecker' forms clumps of grey leaves with up to 15 leaflets and violet flowers in summer. H: 8cm (3in) S: 10cm (4in). Hardiness 4 ☼ ◌

Papaver Poppies are easily recognized with their showy, four-petalled flowers. *P. alpinum* is a dwarf, short-lived perennial with flowers in citrus shades in early summer. H: 15cm (6in) S: 10cm (4in). *P. orientale* 'Patty's Plum' is a robust perennial with flowers of a crushed raspberry shade. H: 1m (3ft) S: 1m (3ft). *P. rhoeas* is the common corn poppy and is an annual with bright red flowers. H: 75cm (30in) S: 60cm (2ft). Hardiness 4 ☼ ◌

Parsley *Petroselinum crispum* is the most commonly used herb and a hardy biennial. The curled-leaved cultivars are widely grown but the flat-leaved sort is often preferred by cooks and is believed to have more flavour.

Passiflora caerulea The exotic flowers of passiflora are produced all summer and are followed by orange, egg-shaped fruit that are edible, though insipid. This climber is hardy in a sheltered, sunny position and climbs by tendrils. The glossy, dark green, hand-shaped leaves are also attractive. H: 8m (30ft). Hardiness 3–4 ☼ ◊ ✗ spring

Peas (*Pisum sativum*) These are weak climbers and most require support. Mangetout peas are picked when immature and eaten whole. Successive sowings give a longer season.

Pelargonium The bedding plants commonly called geraniums are pelargoniums and they are frost-tender plants that will flower almost all year if kept frost-free. They flower most freely if grown in dry soil in full sun. *P.* 'Apple Blossom Rosebud' has fully double, pale and dark pink flowers. H: 40cm (16in) S: 25cm (10in). *P.* 'L'Elégante' is an ivy-leaved cultivar with variegated leaves and single white flowers on trailing growth. H: 20cm (8in) S: 30cm (1ft). Hardiness 1–3 ☼ ◊

Peltandra sagittifolia The glossy, arrowhead-shaped leaves of this hardy aquatic perennial stand elegantly above the water in summer. It will grow in up to 20cm (8in) of water and produces insignificant white 'arum' flowers in early summer. H: 45cm (18in) S: 60cm (2ft). Hardiness 4 ☼

Penstemon These slightly tender small shrubs have colourful tubular flowers in mid- and late summer. All prefer dry soil and full sun and they vary from tiny alpine shrubs to leafy plants. *P.* 'Andenken an Friedrich Hahn' has wine-red flowers. H: 75cm (30in) S: 60cm (2ft). *P.* 'Chester Scarlet' is a large-flowered hybrid with bright red flowers. H: 60cm (2ft) S: 45cm (18in). *P.* 'Evelyn' has narrow leaves and small, pink flowers. H: 45cm (18in) S: 30cm (1ft). *P. newberryi* is a dwarf, evergreen shrub with strident pink flowers. H: 25cm

Penstemon 'Sour Grapes'

Pleioblastus auricomus

(10in) S: 30cm (1ft). *P.* 'Raven' has maroon flowers. H: 75cm (30in) S: 45cm (18in). *P.* 'Sour Grapes' has purple flowers. H: 60cm (2ft) S: 45cm (18in). Hardiness 4 ☼ ◊ ✗ spring

Perovskia 'Blue Spire' This upright, deciduous shrub has white stems and grey, fragrant leaves. In late summer it becomes a haze of tiny blue flowers. It needs a sunny spot and prefers dry soil and should be pruned hard in spring. H: 1.2m (4ft) S: 1m (3ft). Hardiness 4 ☼ ◊ ☁ ❀ ✗ – spring

Persicaria bistorta This robust hardy perennial is semi-evergreen with bright green, broad leaves. The small, pink flowers are produced on tall stems above the foliage in dumpy spikes throughout summer. It tolerates most soils but prefers moist ones. H: 75cm (30in) S: 1m (3ft). Hardiness 4 ☼ ☁ ◖

Petunia These popular bedding plants are tender perennials but best treated as half-hardy annuals. In sunny sites they are covered with flowers all summer in almost every colour, except bright yellow. Grandiflora types have large flowers, Multiflora types have many more smaller flowers, and Floribundas are between the two. Resisto Series have a wide colour range. H: 25cm (10in) S: 30cm (1ft). Hardiness 3 ◊ ❀

Phalaris arundinacea 'Picta' This deciduous, vigorous grass colonizes borders in a variety of soil types. This variegated cultivar has white-striped leaves on erect stems. It thrives in moist soil. The cultivar 'Feesey' has new shoots flushed with pink and is less invasive. H: 1.2m (5ft) S: 1m (3ft). Hardiness 4 ☼ ◖ ◗

Phegopteris hexagonoptera A deciduous fern that spreads by rhizomes and has long-stalked, broad, pinnate fronds of pale green. It thrives in woodland soil or among rocks where the soil does not dry out. H: 45cm (18in) S: 60cm (2ft). Hardiness 4 ☁ ☁

Philadelphus coronarius The mock orange is a large, deciduous shrub with dull green leaves and intensely fragrant white flowers in early summer. It thrives in most soils. The yellow-leaved 'Aureus' may scorch in sun if grown in dry soils. H; 2.5m (8ft) S: 2m (6ft). Hardiness 4 ☼ ☁ ❀ ✗ after flowering

Phlomis fruticosa The grey-leaved phlomis thrive in hot, dry borders. This species is a rounded, evergreen shrub with felted leaves and whorls of golden yellow, tubular flowers in early summer. It is not hardy if grown in rich, moist soil and requires full sun. H: 1m (3ft) S: 1.5m (5ft). Hardiness 4 ☼ ◊ ✗ spring or after flowering

Phlox The five-petalled flowers of phlox are distinctive but the plants vary from tall herbaceous perennials to small evergreen alpines. *P. divaricata* is a spreading, semi-evergreen perennial with lavender or white flowers in early summer. It requires moist, woodland conditions. H: 35cm (14in) S: 45cm (18in). *P. paniculata* is a herbaceous perennial, 'Amethyst' has lilac flowers and 'Sandringham' is pale pink with deep eyes. H: 1.2m (4ft) S: 45cm (18in). *P. stolonifera* is a creeping woodland plant. H: 15cm (6in) S: 30cm (1ft). *P. subulata* is a mossy evergreen with small flowers in early summer. It requires well-drained soil and sun. H: 10cm (4in) S: 45cm (18in). Hardiness 4 ☼ ☁ ◊ ●

Phormium tenax The New Zealand flaxes are bold, evergreen foliage plants with fibrous, narrow, upright leaves. Established plants produce tall stems of tubular, dark red flowers in summer. Phormiums prefer moist, well-drained soil and full sun. In cold inland gardens they may be damaged by frost but they tolerate coastal winds. *P. tenax* Purpureum Group has purple leaves. H: 3m (10ft) S: 2.5m (8ft). Hardiness 4 ☼ ◊

Picea The spruces include many forest trees that would not be suitable for gardens, and the common Christmas tree (*P. abies*). Some of the dwarf cultivars of the large species are interesting evergreen shrubs for the garden and thrive in most soils, in full sun. *P. glauca* var. *albertiana* 'Conica' forms a neat cone of dense foliage in time. H: 2m (6ft) S: 1m (3ft). *P. mariana* 'Nana' is a dense dwarf shrub with blue-green needles. H: 45cm (18in) S: 45cm (18in). Hardiness 4 ☼ ⚔

Pieris These evergreen shrubs are woodland plants that prefer moist, humus-rich soil and light shade and shelter, and need acid conditions. They are grown for their bright red young foliage and clusters of white or pink urn-shaped flowers in spring. They can be grown in large pots and tubs. *P. formosa* var. *forrestii* 'Wakehurst' has bright red foliage and white flowers. H: 2.5m (8ft) S: 2.5m (8ft). *P. japonica* 'Firecrest' has deep green leaves, red when young. H: 2m (6ft) S: 2m (6ft). Hardiness 4 ☼ ☁

Pilosella aurantiaca This creeping perennial makes extensive mats of hairy green rosettes, and in summer it produces tall stems covered with black hairs with clusters of bright, rusty orange, dandelion-like flowers. It is easy to grow in any soil but can be invasive. H: 20cm (8in) S: 1m (3ft). Hardiness 4 ☼ ☁ ◊ ✼

Pittosporum tenuifolium This evergreen shrub has thin, black branches and small, glossy, wavy-edged leaves. In early summer the deep chocolate-purple flowers open and scent the air. It may be damaged by frost in inland gardens and needs a sheltered spot. H: 6m (20ft) S: 3m (10ft). 'Silver Queen' is compact with white-edged leaves. H: 4m (13ft) S: 2m (6ft). Hardiness 4 ☼ ◊ ✿ ⚔ spring

Plantago major 'Rosularis' The common lawn plantain would not be permitted in any but the most wildlife-oriented garden but this ornamental form is attractive because the stringy summer flower spikes have become large rose-like structures in bright green. It is a hardy perennial and will self-seed. In dry soil it is prone to mildew. H: 25cm (10in) S: 30cm (1ft). Hardiness 4 ☼ ☁

Pleioblastus auricomus Some bamboos are invasive but this species has short rhizomes and makes large clumps and is rarely a

Pontedera cordata

nuisance. It is evergreen with purple stems and narrow leaves striped green and gold and makes striking, tall ground cover in moist soil out of strong winds. H: 1.2m (4ft) S: 1.5m (5ft). Hardiness 4 ☼ ☁

Polemonium caeruleum This hardy perennial forms clumps of green, finely divided leaves and tall spikes of pale blue flowers in early summer. It will adapt to most gardens and is easy to grow from seed. H: 75cm (30in) S: 30cm (1ft). Hardiness 4 ☼ ☁

Polygonatum These hardy, rhizomatous perennials are grown for their graceful foliage, arching habit and pendulous flowers from late spring. They are adaptable but prefer light shade and moist, woodland conditions. Solomon's seal sawfly can strip plants of leaves. *P.* x *hybridum* has clusters of four flowers under the leaves. H: 1.2m (4ft) S: 45cm (18in). *P. verticillatum* has whorls of narrow leaves and slender flowers. H: 75cm (30in) S: 25cm (10in). Hardiness 4 ☼ ☁

Polypodium vulgare The common polypody has feather-shaped, evergreen fronds that arise from the creeping rhizomes at soil level. It grows in well-drained, moist soil or may creep up trees and walls in mild, moist areas. There are ornamental cultivars with crested or finely divided fronds. H: 30cm (1ft) S: 60cm (2ft). Hardiness 4 ☼ ☁ ◊ ◊

Polystichum These evergreen ferns have rosettes of large fronds, often finely divided and with rusty scales along the midribs. Although evergreen the old fronds should be cut away in spring as the new growth emerges. They prefer moist soil and shade. *P. acrostichoides* has dark green leaves. H: 45cm (18in) S: 1m (3ft). *P. aculeatum* is reliably evergreen. H: 60cm (2ft) S: 75cm (30in). *P. setiferum* 'Pulcherrimum Bevis' has an elegant habit and fine fronds. H: 60cm (2ft) S: 75cm (30in). Hardiness 4 ☁ ☁

Pontederia cordata This pond perennial has tall stems of glossy, lance-shaped foliage and spikes of small blue flowers in late summer. It will grow in moist soil or in up to 10cm (4in) of water. It requires full sun. H: 1m (3ft) S: 60cm (2ft). Hardiness 4 ☼ ●

Potentilla fruticosa This is a compact, twiggy, deciduous bush with finely divided leaves and small, rose-like flowers throughout summer in shades of yellow, white and orange and salmon. They are hardy and flourish in poor and dry soil and tolerate cold, windy gardens. H: 75cm (30in) S: 1.2m (4ft). Hardiness 4 ☼ ☁ ◊ ☒ – spring

Pratia pedunculata The mats of tiny green leaves of this hardy perennial are studded with pale blue, starry flowers in summer. It prefers average soil and light shade, and may be invasive, covering large areas of rock gardens, paving or gravel gardens. H: 2cm (1in) S: 60cm (2ft). Hardiness 4 ☼ ☁

Primula This huge genus contains a great diversity of plants from bog perennials to alpines. Most flower in spring and early summer. *P. beesiana* is a deep pink candelabra primula for moist soil. H: 60cm (2ft) S: 60cm (2ft). *P. denticulata* is the drumstick primula with round heads of purple, pink or white flowers. H: 45cm (18in) S: 45cm (18in). *P. elatior* is the oxlip with pale yellow flowers. H: 30cm (1ft) S: 25cm (10in). *P. gracilipes* has purple flowers and requires alpine conditions. H: 10cm (4in) S: 20cm (8in). *P. marginata* 'Linda Pope' has evergreen rosettes and mauve flowers. H: 15cm (6in) S: 30cm (1ft). *P. prolifera* is a candelabra type with bright yellow flowers. H: 60cm (2ft) S: 60cm (2ft). *P. pulverulenta* is a candelabra type with magenta flowers. H: 1m (3ft) S: 60cm (2ft). *P. rosea* needs moist soil and has strident pink flowers. H: 20cm (8in) S: 20cm (8in). *P. veris* is the cowslip with small, deep yellow flowers. H: 25cm (10in) S: 25cm (10in). *P. vulgaris* is the primrose with pale yellow flowers. H: 20cm (8in) S: 30cm (1ft). *P. whitei* has compact bunches of delft blue flowers and needs cool, acid conditions. H: 15cm (6in) S: 20cm (8in). Hardiness 4 ☼ ☁ ꕥ ●

Prunus This genus includes peaches, cherries and plums as well as ornamental plants. Most are hardy shrubs or trees and may be evergreen or deciduous. *P. laurocerasus* is the evergreen cherry laurel with spikes of white flowers in spring. H: 8m (25ft) S: 10m (33ft). *P. tenella* is the dwarf

almond and is a low, deciduous shrub with deep pink flowers in spring. H: 1.5m (5ft) S: 1.5m (5ft). Hardiness 4 ☼ ☁ ◊ ☒ after flowering

Pterocephalus perennis The mauve flowers of this dwarf, evergreen perennial are produced in summer. It is suitable for rock gardens or paving. H: 8cm (3in) S: 20cm (8in). Hardiness 4 ☼ ◊ ꕥ

Pulmonaria These deciduous or evergreen herbaceous perennials have early flowers in pinks and blues. All make good ground cover. *P. angustifolia* has plain green leaves and blue flowers. H: 25cm (10in) S: 45cm (18in). 'Munstead Blue' is similar, while *P. longifolia* has spotted leaves. H: 30cm (1ft) S: 45cm (18in). *P. officinalis* has spotted leaves and blue flowers that open pink. H: 25cm (10in) S: 45cm (18in). Hardiness 4 ☼ ☁

Pulsatilla The pasque flowers are perennials of dry grassland with silky-haired, fine leaves and large goblet-shaped flowers in spring. They require well-drained soil and full sun and dislike disturbance. *P. vernalis* has white flowers, flushed with violet. H: 15cm (6in) S: 10cm (4in). *P. vulgaris* has slightly nodding, purple flowers. H: 15cm (6in) S: 20cm (8in). *P. vulgaris* var. *rubra* has red flowers. H: 15cm (6in) S: 20cm (8in). Hardiness 4 ☼ ◊

Punica granatum var. *nana* This dwarf variety of the pomegranate is a pretty bush with small, glossy leaves which turn yellow in autumn before they fall. The funnel-shaped, scarlet flowers are borne in summer and small fruit may form. It is not reliably frost-hardy and needs a warm sunny place by a wall in cold climates, or can be grown in pots. H: 60cm (2ft) S: 60cm (2ft). Hardiness 2–4 ☼ ◊

Pyracantha 'Orange Glow' This thorny evergreen shrub can be grown as a wall shrub or a hedge. The white flowers in spring are followed by orange berries. It will tolerate a variety of soils. H: 3m (10ft) S: 3m (10ft). Hardiness 4 ☼ ☁ ◊ ꕥ ☒ – spring

Ramonda myconi It is hard to believe that this evergreen perennial is hardy: when in flower, in early summer, it looks like an African violet with purple flowers. Its crinkly,

hairy leaves form flat rosettes and it is best grown in vertical crevices in walls so that the rosettes do not fill with water in winter. It requires moist but well-drained soil. H: 10cm (4in) S: 20cm (8in). Hardiness 4 ☁

Ranunculus The buttercups include hardy and tender plants, and herbaceous perennials, annuals and tuberous plants. Most have white or yellow flowers with glossy petals and some can be invasive weeds. *R. acris* is the meadow buttercup with coarsely divided leaves and tall, branched stems of bright yellow flowers. *R. acris* 'Flore Pleno' has tightly double flowers. H: 60cm (2ft) S: 45cm (18in). *R. flammula* is a pondside plant that prefers moist soil and has bright yellow flowers in early summer. H: 75cm (30in) S: 60cm (2ft). *R. lingua* is a marginal aquatic with narrow leaves and yellow flowers in early summer. H: 1.5m (5ft) S: 2m (6ft). Hardiness 4 ☼ ☁ ●

Reseda These are hardy perennials or annuals with spreading stems and clusters of tiny flowers. They like dry, sunny, alkaline soils. *R. lutea* is a perennial with pale yellow, scentless flowers in summer. H: 30cm (1ft) S: 30cm (1ft). *R. odorata* is mignonette, an annual with fragrant small flowers at the end of the shoots. H: 45cm (16in) S: 20cm (8in). Hardiness 4 ☼ ◊ ꕥ ꕥ

Rheum palmatum

Rhamnus alaternus The Italian buckthorn is an upright evergreen shrub with dark stems and small, dark green leaves. The yellow flowers in spring are followed by black, poisonous berries in autumn. In cold areas it should be grown against a sunny wall. 'Argenteovariegata' has white-edged leaves. H: 5m (15ft) S: 4m (13ft). Hardiness 4 ☼ ◊ ✤

Rheum palmatum The Chinese rhubarb is a hardy perennial with a thick rootstock and large, deeply cut leaves and tall, branched spikes of tiny pink or red flowers in early summer. It prefers moist, rich soil and thrives beside ponds. H: 2m (6ft) S: 2m (6ft). Hardiness 4 ☼ ☁ ▮

Rhinanthus major The greater yellow rattle is an annual semi-parasite that may be grown in the wild garden among grasses on which it relies. In summer it produces yellow, tubular flowers among the yellow bracts. H: 30cm (1ft) S: 15cm (6in). Hardiness 4 ☼ ◊

Rhodanthemum hosmariense This spreading, shrubby plant forms a carpet of feathery, silver leaves, and thrives in dry soil in full sun. All summer it produces short-stemmed white, daisy-like flowers. It is a reliable plant for gravel gardens and paving. H: 15cm (6in) S: 30cm (1ft). Hardiness 3 ☼ ◊

Rhodiola rosea This fleshy perennial forms domes of purple stems with blue-green leaves and in summer has small clusters of tiny yellow-green flowers. It thrives in average or dry soil in full sun, at the front of borders or in rock gardens. H: 40cm (16in) S: 40cm (16in). Hardiness 4 ☼ ◊ ✤

Rhododendron Rhododendrons are lime-hating, evergreen shrubs that vary from small shrubs to large, tree-like specimens. Although grown mainly for their late spring flowers many have attractive foliage. They thrive in moist, partially shaded sites. *R. cinnabarinum* has metallic, blue-green leaves and pendulous, tubular, reddish flowers. H: 6m (20ft) S: 2m (6ft). *R.* 'Curlew' is a dwarf hybrid with yellow flowers. H: 60cm (2ft) S: 60cm (2ft). *R.* 'Fabia' has orange-pink flowers. H: 2m (6ft) S: 2m (6ft). *R. williamsianum* has abundant pink flowers and tolerates full sun. H: 1.5m

Rosa 'Ballerina'

Rosa rugosa 'Alba'

(5ft) S: 1.2m (4ft). *R. yakushimanum* is a dwarf plant with pale pink flowers. H: 2m (6ft) S: 2m (6ft). Hardiness 4 ☁

Rhodohypoxis baurii This slightly tender bulb forms clumps of grassy leaves with masses of starry pink and red flowers in summer. It thrives in humus-rich, moist but well-drained compost. Protect plants from winter wet by covering them with glass. H: 10cm (4in) S: 10cm (4in). Hardiness 3-4 ☼

Ribes laurifolium The sprawling branches of this evergreen shrub are clothed with coarsely toothed, deep green, glossy leaves and in early spring the drooping clusters of pale green flowers open. Male and female flowers are produced on separate plants and the males have longer flower spikes. It is a useful shrub for moist soil. H: 1m (5ft) S: 1m (5ft). Hardiness 4 ☼ ☁ ⋏ after flowering

Ricinus communis 'Impala' This tender shrub is the source of castor oil, but the seeds and the plant are toxic. In cold climates it is usually grown as a tender annual and is valued for its large, lobed, purple leaves and curious spiny seed pods. It is a good foliage plant for summer bedding, when it will reach 1.2m (4ft), or heated greenhouses. H: 5m (16ft) S: 4m (13ft). Hardiness 1–3 ☼

Robinia hispida This suckering shrub has bristly, brittle branches and is usually grown against a wall to provide support. In sun on dry soil the finely divided foliage is augmented by pendulous clusters of deep rose 'pea' flowers in early summer. H: 2.5m (8ft) S: 3m (10ft). Hardiness 4 ☼ ◊ ⋏ – after flowering

Romneya coulteri In late summer the coarsely lobed, blue-green leaves of this suckering, woody perennial are interspersed with large, white, yellow-centred flowers. In light soil in full sun this slightly tender plant will thrive. H: 1.5m (5ft) S: 2m (6ft). Hardiness 3 ☼ ◊

Rosa Most roses prefer rich soil that does not dry out in summer and full sun. Where rust and black spot are prevalent, roses should be sprayed from late spring. *R.* 'Ballerina' has pale pink, single flowers. H: 1.5m (5ft) S: 1.2m (4ft). *R.* 'Camaïeux' has double pink flowers. H: 80cm (32in) S: 80cm (32in). *R.* 'Cardinal de Richelieu' has double, burgundy flowers. H: 1m (3ft) S: 1.2m (4ft). *R.* 'Charles de Mills' has double, pink flowers. H: 1.2m (4ft) S: 1.2m (4ft). *R.* 'Climbing Cécile Brünner' has small, pale pink flowers. H: 6m (20ft). *R.* 'Fantin Latour' has double, pale pink flowers. H: 1.5m (5ft)

S: 1.2m (4ft). *R. gallica* 'Versicolor' has pink and white-striped flowers. H: 80cm (30in) S: 1.2m (4ft). *R. glauca* has purple foliage and pink flowers. H: 2m (6ft) S: 1.5m (5ft). *R.* 'Great Maiden's Blush' has grey leaves and pale pink flowers. H: 2m (6ft) S: 1.2m (4ft). *R.* Highfield is a climber with salmon flowers. H: 3m (10ft). *R.* x *jacksonii* 'Max Graf' has single, pink flowers. H: 60cm (2ft) S: 2.5m (8ft). *R.* 'Marchesa Boccella' has double, deep pink flowers. H: 1.2m (4ft) S: 1m (3ft). *R.* Margaret Merril has pure white flowers. H: 80m (32in) S: 60cm (2ft). *R.* 'Mevrouw Nathalie Nypels' has pale pink flowers. H: 75cm (30in) S: 60cm (2ft). *R. mulliganii* is a climber with single, white flowers. H: 6m (20ft). *R.* x *odorata* 'Mutabilis' has single flowers in red and apricot. H: 3m (10ft) S: 6m (6ft). *R. pimpinellifolia* has spiny stems and white flowers. H: 1m (3ft) S: 1.2m (4ft). *R.* 'Robert le Diable' has purple flowers. H: 1m (3ft) S: 1m (3ft). *R. rubiginosa* has pale pink flowers and scented leaves. H: 2.5m (8ft) S: 2.5m (8ft). *R. rugosa* has single pink flowers and showy hips; 'Alba' has white flowers. H: 2m (6ft) S: 2m (6ft). *R.* 'Tour de Malakoff' has purple-violet flowers. H: 2m (6ft) S: 1.5m (5ft). *R.* 'William Lobb' has purple and lavender, double blooms. H: 2m (6ft) S: 2m (6ft). Hardiness 4 ☼ ⊛ ⋇ spring

Rosmarinus officinalis This evergreen shrub is the herb rosemary and has silvery-green foliage and pale blue flowers in spring. H: 1.5m (5ft) S: 1.5m (5ft). 'Aureus' has gold-splashed foliage and is weaker-growing. 'Benenden Blue' has deep blue flowers. 'Sissinghurst Blue' is upright with rich blue flowers. Hardiness 4 ☼ ◊ ⊛ ⋇ ⋇ spring

Runner beans *Phaseolus coccineus* is a tender, twining plant with red flowers. It likes moist, rich soil and plants produce large crops if the beans are picked while young.

Ruta graveolens This shrubby herb has pungent, blue-green, finely divided foliage and pale yellow flowers in summer. The plant has no culinary value and the sap from foliage can cause severe blisters. H: 1m (3ft) S: 75cm (30in). 'Jackman's Blue' has foliage of a more striking shade. H: 60cm (2ft) S: 75cm (30in). Hardiness 4 ☼ ◊ ⋇ - spring

Salix caprea

Sagittaria sagittifolia This marginal aquatic perennial will grow in moist soil or in water up to 25cm (10in) deep. The leaves under water are narrow but those above the surface are arrow-shaped and deep, glossy green. The three-petalled, white flowers are carried above the leaves in summer. H: 75cm (30in) S: 1m (3ft). Hardiness 4 ☼

Salix The willows are a diverse group of shrubs and trees but most grow rapidly and they all bear catkins in spring. A few are small shrubs suitable for the rock garden. *S. caprea* is the goat willow. It has ornamental cultivars but the species is good in wild gardens. H: 6m (20ft) S: 5m (16ft). *S. exigua* has narrow grey leaves and thrives on dry soil. H: 4m (13ft) S: 5m (16ft). *S. lanata* is a rounded bush with grey leaves. H: 1m (3ft) S: 5m (16ft). Hardiness 4 ☼ ☁ ◊ ● ⋇ ⋇ - winter

Salvia This genus is extremely varied, and contains annuals, biennials, perennials and shrubs that are tender or frost-hardy, but most have whorls of lipped flowers in summer and square stems with aromatic foliage. *S. farinacea* is usually grown as a tender bedding annual and 'Victoria' has deep blue flowers. H: 45cm (18in) S: 30cm (1ft). *S. officinalis* is sage, an evergreen, dwarf shrub

Saxifraga fortunei

that thrives in dry soil. H: 80cm (32in) S: 1m (3ft). *S. officinalis* Purpurascens Group has purple leaves. *S. pratensis* is a hardy perennial with branched spikes of lavender flowers. H: 1m (3ft) S: 45cm (18in). *S. nemorosa* 'Ostfriesland' is perennial with purple flowers. H: 45cm (18in) S: 60cm (2ft). *S. sclarea* var. *turkestanica* is biennial with pink stems of pale flowers. H: 1m (3ft) S: 45cm (18in). *S.* x *superba* is perennial with purple flowers in late summer. H: 60cm (2ft) S: 60cm (2ft). *S.* x *sylvestris* is perennial with violet flowers in late summer. H: 80cm (32in) S: 30cm (1ft). Hardiness 4 ☼ ◊ ⊛ ⋇ ⋇ - spring

Sambucus nigra 'Guincho Purple' This deciduous shrub is a cultivar of the common elder. The leaves are dark purple and in summer it produces flat heads of pink flowers. It colours best in full sun, and can be pruned to keep it small. H: 4m (13ft) S: 5m (16ft). Hardiness 4 ☼ ☁ ◊ ⋇ - spring

Sanguinaria canadensis This hardy perennial has scalloped, blue-grey leaves and delicate, white, poppy-like flowers in spring. These last only a day or so but the flowers of the double forma *multiplex* last a little longer. It requires moist, humus-rich soil. H: 15cm (6in) S: 60cm (2ft). Hardiness 4 ☁

Sanguisorba minor This perennial has greenish, fluffy flowerheads on wiry, stiff stems above divided, blue-green leaves. It is suitable for a wild garden, flowering in summer. H: 60cm (2ft) S: 60cm (2ft). Hardiness 4 ☼ ◊ ✿

Santolina These dwarf, evergreen shrubs have aromatic, feathery leaves in grey and green and small, round, yellow flowers. They are suitable for edging. *S. chamaecyparissus* is cotton lavender, with grey leaves and yellow flowers in summer. H: 50cm (20in) S: 60cm (2ft). *S. pinnata* has green leaves and cream flowers. H: 75cm (30in) S: 60cm (2ft). Hardiness 4 ☼ ◊ ✿ ⋀ - spring

Saponaria ocymoides Called tumbling Ted, this spreading perennial is suitable for rock gardens and raised beds where the flowering stems will cascade over the edge. It produces massed, rich pink flowers in summer. H: 8cm (3in) S: 60cm (2ft). Hardiness 4 ☼ ◊

Sarcococca These evergreen shrubs have small dark green leaves. In winter the cream, scented flowers open, followed by red or black berries that ripen the following year. *S. hookeriana* var. *humilis* spreads by suckering stems and has black berries. H: 60cm (2ft) S: 1m (3ft). *S. ruscifolia* has red berries. H: 1m (3ft) S: 1m (3ft). Hardiness 4 ☁ ☁ ✿ ⋀

Saururus cernuus This perennial bog plant has heart-shaped leaves on erect stems and curved spikes of tiny, white, fragrant flowers in early summer that give it the name of lizard's tail. H: 45cm (18in) S: 60cm (2ft). Hardiness 4 ☼ ✿

Saxifraga This is a huge genus but the most popular are alpine species that require full sun and well-drained soil. Most are evergreen perennials with leaves in rosettes and small, five-petalled flowers. *S. cochlearis* has green leaves encrusted with lime and red-spotted, white flowers in early summer. H: 20cm (8in) S: 15cm (6in). *S. fortunei* requires moist, semi-shaded soil, and flowers in late summer. H: 30cm (1ft) S: 30cm (1ft). *S. longifolia* has long stems with massed white flowers in summer. H: 60cm (2ft) S: 20cm (8in). *S. paniculata* has grey leaves and white flowers

in summer. H: 15cm (6in) S: 25cm (10in). *S.* 'Southside Seedling' has arching stems of white, red-spotted flowers in early summer. H: 30cm (1ft) S: 20cm (8in). *S.* 'Tumbling Waters' has arching, branched stems of white flowers. H: 45cm (18in) S: 30cm (1ft). *S.* x *urbium* is a low, evergreen perennial with white, red-spotted flowers. H: 30cm (1ft) S: 60cm (2ft). Hardiness 4 ☼ ◊

Scabiosa columbaria This hardy perennial has divided leaves and lilac flowerheads on branched stems above the leaves in late summer. H: 60cm (2ft) S: 1m (3ft). The most common garden forms are S. 'Butterfly Blue' and S. 'Pink Mist'. H: 40cm (16in) S: 40cm (16in). Hardiness 4 ☼ ◊ ✿

Schoenoplectus lacustris This plant for moist soil has little value except for wildlife but subsp. *tabernaemontani* 'Zebrinus' has stripes across its green stems. H: 1m (3ft) S: 60cm (2ft). Hardiness 4 ☼ ◆

Scilla siberica The Siberian squill is a hardy bulb that flowers in early spring. It will self-seed in well-drained soil. Each bulb produces several stems with up to five bell-shaped flowers of rich blue. In 'Spring Beauty' they are a deeper shade. H: 15cm (6in) S: 10cm (4in). Hardiness 4 ☼ ☁ ◊

Scrophularia auriculata This hardy perennial prefers moist soil, and will grow beside ponds. The large leaves make a dense clump and the deep maroon, small flowers in late summer are useful for insects. 'Variegata' has bold white margins to the leaves. H: 1m (3ft) S: 75cm (30in). Hardiness 4 ☼ ☁ ✿

Sedum Some of these fleshy perennials are suitable for the rock garden. *S. acre* is an invasive, low carpeter with yellow flowers. H: 5cm (2in) S: 60cm (2ft). *S.* 'Herbstfreude' has deep pink flowers. H: 60cm (2ft) S: 60cm (2ft). *S. spectabile* has blue-green leaves and pink flowers. H: 45cm (18in) S: 45cm (18in). *S. telephium* subsp. *maximum* 'Atropurpureum' has purple stems and leaves and pink flowers in summer. H: 60cm (2ft) S: 45cm (18in). *S.* 'Vera Jameson' has purple leaves and pink flowers in late summer. H: 20cm (8in) S: 45cm (18in). Hardiness 4 ☼ ◊ ✿

Sempervivum The houseleeks are fleshy, hardy perennials that form clusters of rosettes. Each rosette produces a stem of starry flowers and then dies, to be replaced by offsets. They are suitable for rock gardens and dry-stone walls. *S. arachnoideum* has small rosettes covered with 'cobwebs', and pink flowers. H: 8cm (3in) S: 30cm (1ft). *S. montanum* has dull green leaves and red flowers. H: 10cm (4in) S: 30cm (1ft). Hardiness 4 ☼ ◊

Senecio This huge genus contains plants of all kinds, but most are small shrubs with silver leaves and small daisy-like flowers. *S. cineraria* is a slightly tender silver-leaved shrub with golden flowers suitable for sun and dry soil. H: 60cm (2ft) S: 60cm (2ft). *S. smithii* is a robust perennial for moist soil with large white daisies appearing in summer. H: 1.2m (4ft) S: 60cm (2ft). *S. viravira* is a sprawling, slightly tender shrub with finely cut silver leaves and pale yellow tassel flowers. H: 60cm (2ft) S: 1m (3ft). Hardiness 3–4 ☼ ☁ ◊ ◆ ⋀

Shortia soldanelloides This evergreen, low-growing, rhizomatous perennial has rounded, glossy leaves and pink, fringed flowers in spring. It is hardy but new shoots may be frosted in cold areas. It needs humus-rich, moist, acid soil. H: 20cm (8in) S: 25cm (10in). Hardiness 4 ☁

Sedum 'Herbstfreude'

Sidalcea 'William Smith' This clump-forming perennial has glossy, round leaves, deeply cut on the flowering stems, and thrives in most soils and in sun or partial shade. The deep, rose-pink flowers are carried on erect, thin stems in summer and resemble miniature hollyhocks. H: 1m (3ft) S: 45cm (18in). Hardiness 4 ☼ ☁

Silene Campions are varied annuals and perennials, most of which are frost-hardy and thrive in full sun and dry soil. All have colourful flowers in shades of pink or white (occasionally lilac) with five petals. *S. dioica* is the pink campion with evergreen clumps of leaves and pale pink flowers in early summer. H: 75cm (30in) S: 60cm (2ft). 'Flore Pleno' has double flowers. *S. fimbriata* has white, heavily laced petals and large, inflated calyces. H: 60cm (2ft) S: 60cm (2ft). *S. virginica* is the fire pink, a rock garden perennial with bright red flowers in early summer. H: 30cm (1ft) S: 30cm (1ft). Hardiness 4 ☼ ◊

Sisyrinchium These perennials have grassy clumps of foliage and slim spikes of starry flowers in summer. They grow rapidly from seed and most prefer moist, but well-drained soil and full sun. Some are slightly tender and they resent winter wet. *S. californicum* Brachypus Group has yellow flowers. H: 45cm (18in) S: 15cm (6in). *S. 'E. K. Balls'* is compact, with purple flowers. H: 25cm (10in) S: 15cm (6in). *S. graminoides* is called blue-eyed grass and has small blue flowers. H: 45cm (18in) S: 15cm (6in). *S. striatum* forms clumps of fans of grey leaves with tall spikes of pale yellow flowers. H: 75cm (30in) S: 25cm (10in). Hardiness 4 ☼ ◊

Sium sisarum This is an ancient vegetable, known as skirret, with edible, thick roots. It is a perennial with dark green, coarsely divided foliage and umbels of white flowers in summer. It is useful in the wild garden. H: 1.2m (4ft) S: 45cm (18in). Hardiness 4 ☼ ✺

Skimmia japonica 'Rubella' Skimmias are valued for their dense evergreen foliage and red berries in winter. They make neat, dome-shaped bushes and the male and female flowers are produced on separate plants. This

is a male cultivar that pollinates female plants and has red buds in winter that open to white, fragrant flowers in spring. Skimmias prefer acid soil. H: 1m (3ft) S: 1m (3ft). Hardiness 4 ☁ ☁ ⊛ ✂ spring if necessary

Smilacina racemosa This hardy herbaceous plant has erect stems with rounded, dark green leaves in two rows along their length. In early summer the stems are topped with heads of fluffy, white, scented flowers and these may be followed by small, red berries. It prefers moist soil and part shade. H: 1m (3ft) S: 60cm (2ft). Hardiness 4 ☁ ☁ ⊛

Smyrnium perfoliatum This hardy biennial produces a rosette of deep green leaves in the first year, and in the following spring it produces a ridged stem of tiny yellow flowers. These are surrounded by lime-green bracts that make a showy display for many weeks before the plants set seed. It is useful in mixed borders and in the wild garden. H: 1m (3ft) S: 30cm (1ft). Hardiness 4 ☼ ☁

Soft fruit This term includes those not grown on trees. These are the cane fruit such as blackberries and raspberries, strawberries, and those that grow on small bushes such as redcurrants and gooseberries. Most require fertile soil and full sun to crop well, though gooseberries will tolerate some shade.

Smyrnium perfoliatum

Solanum This huge group of plants includes the potato (*S. tuberosum*), but although the plant form varies the flowers are very distinctive. They are usually purple or white with five points and have a central, yellow beak. Most are rather tender, though fast-growing. *S. crispum* is often called the potato vine because of its flowers and is a scrambler for a sheltered, sunny spot with purple flowers all summer. H: 6m (20ft). The cultivar 'Glasnevin' has deep purple flowers. *S. jasminoides* 'Album' is a weak scrambler with small white flowers all summer. H: 6m (20ft). Hardiness 3–4 ☼ ◊ ✂ - spring

Soldanella villosa In the woodland garden, with humus-rich soil, this creeping, hardy perennial will form dense clumps of small, rounded leaves. In spring the erect stems of nodding, purple, fringed, bell-shaped flowers are produced. H: 30cm (1ft) S: 20cm (8in). Hardiness 4 ☁

Soleirolia soleirolii This creeping perennial can be a nuisance in mild climates where it forms congested mats of translucent stems covered with tiny, green leaves. It prefers moist soil and will not thrive in dry conditions. There are cultivars with yellow and variegated leaves. The tiny flowers have no beauty. H: 5cm (2in) S: 1m (3ft). Hardiness 3–4 ☁ ☁ ◗

Solidago odora The perennial golden rods are grown for their feathery heads of yellow flowers on tall stems in summer, often into autumn. *S. odora* has unbranched stems with narrow leaves that are scented of aniseed. The tiny yellow flowers are produced in pyramidal heads and last many weeks. It tolerates dry soil and prefers sun. H: 60cm (2ft) S: 45cm (18in). Hardiness 4 ☼ ◊ ⊛

Sorbus These hardy, decidous shrubs are grown for their handsome leaves, white or pale pink flowers and yellow, red, white or pink berries in autumn. *S. hupehensis* is a small tree with divided blue-green leaves and pink-flushed, white berries. H: 8m (25ft) S: 8m (25ft). *S. reducta* is a suckering shrub with bright red autumn colour and crimson berries that turn white later. H: 1.2m (4ft) S: 2m (6ft). Hardiness 4 ☼ ✺ ✂

Spartium junceum The Spanish broom is a
hardy, drought-tolerant shrub with green
stems and tiny leaves. The masses of bright
yellow, fragrant, pea-shaped flowers open in
summer along the young shoots. It is easy to
grow from seed. H: 3m (10ft) S: 2m (6ft).
Hardiness 4 ☼ ◊ ⊗ ⋏ – after flowering

Stachys These herbaceous perennials have
whorls of tubular flowers in summer and
often aromatic leaves. Most prefer full sun
and many have grey, hairy leaves. *S. byzantina*
is a low, spreading evergreen with spikes of
mauve flowers in summer, 'Cotton Boll' has
spherical clusters of bracts on the flowers
stems. H: 45cm (18in) S: 60cm (2ft).
S. officinalis is a hairy perennial with upright
stems of purple flowers. H: 60cm (2ft)
S: 30cm (1ft). *S. palustris* is a creeping
perennial with stems of mauve flowers. It
prefers moist soil, H: 75cm (30in) S: 60cm
(2ft). Hardiness 4 ☼ ☁ ◊ ● ❀

Stellaria These weak-stemmed perennials
have narrow leaves and white, starry flowers
in summer. These species are useful for wild
gardens and meadows. *S. graminea* is the
lesser stitchwort from dry, acid soils. H: 30cm
(1ft) S: 15cm (6in). *S. holostea* is the greater
stitchwort with white flowers in summer that
thrives in semi-shade. H: 45cm (18in) S:
30cm (1ft). Hardiness 4 ☼ ☁ ◊ ❀

Stokesia laevis This hardy perennial forms
evergreen clumps and grows best in moist,
well-drained acid soil and may die in wet
soil in winter. In summer it produces stems
each with a single, blue-and-purple bloom.
These last well in the garden and as cut
flowers. H: 60cm (2ft) S: 45cm (18in).
Hardiness 4 ☼ ◊

Stratiotes aloides The water soldier is a
floating aquatic perennial with a rosette of
narrow, spiny leaves. In winter the plants sink
to the bottom of the pond, but in summer
they rise again and the small white flowers
are produced. It increases by short runners.
H: 30cm (1ft) S: 30cm (1ft). Hardiness 4 ☼

Strobilanthes atropurpureus This large hardy
perennial has large, toothed, dark green
leaves and clusters of tubular purple flowers

Solanum jasminoides 'Album'

at the ends of the erect shoots in late summer.
H: 1.2m (4ft) S: 1m (3ft). Hardiness 4 ☼ ◊

Succisa pratensis This hardy perennial forms
clumps of hairy leaves with violet flowers in
late summer. It will grow in poor soil that is
not too dry and is very useful in wild gardens.
H: 45cm (18in) S: 60cm (2ft). Hardiness 4 ☼
◊ ❀

Symphytum ibericum This rhizomatous,
hardy perennial forms clumps of coarse, hairy
leaves and in early summer produces clusters
of pale yellow flowers that open from red
buds. It is useful ground cover in light shade
and in heavy soil. H: 45cm (18in) S: 60cm
(2ft). Hardiness 4 ☼ ☁ ◊ ● ❀

Tamarix ramosissima The tamarisk is a useful
large shrub for coastal areas as the flexible
branches and small leaves withstand wind and
salt spray. In late summer there are masses of
tiny pale pink flowers. It tolerates most soils
including poor, dry ones. H: 5m (16ft) S: 4m
(13ft). Hardiness 4 ☼ ◊ ⋏ – in spring

Tanacetum This genus contains hardy
herbaceous perennials, dwarf, silver leaved
shrubs and the herb feverfew. They have
aromatic foliage which may cause skin
irritation. *T. densum* subsp. *amani* forms an

Stokesia laevis

evergreen mound of finely divided silver
foliage with yellow flowers. It thrives in dry,
sunny sites. H: 25cm (10in) S: 30cm (1ft).
T. parthenium 'Aureum' is the golden-leaved
feverfew, a short-lived woody perennial with
aromatic foliage and clusters of white daisy
flowers in summer. H: 45cm (18in) S: 30cm
(1ft). *T. vulgare* var. *crispum* is the curled-
leaved form of the common tansy, a stout
perennial with heads of small, yellow flowers
in summer. H: 75cm (30in) S: 60cm (2ft).
Hardiness 4 ☼ ◊ ⊗

Taraxacum officinale The dandelion is a
short-lived perennial with rosettes of jagged-
toothed leaves and bright yellow flowers in
early summer. It can be a weed but is also a
useful plant for insects and the blanched
leaves are tasty addition to salads. H: 25cm
(10in) S: 20cm (8in). Hardiness 4 ☼ ☁ ◊

Tellima grandiflora This herbaceous
perennial forms mounds of rounded,
scalloped leaves and thrives in woodland
conditions though it is drought-tolerant and
makes good ground cover in shade. In early
summer the tall spikes of small, greenish-
white flowers are produced. *T. grandiflora*
Rubra Group has purple-tinged foliage.
H: 75cm (30in) S: 30cm (1ft). Hardiness 4
☁ ☁ ◊

Thalictrum delavayi This elegant, hardy perennial forms clumps by spreading with short rhizomes, and has blue-green foliage. In summer it produces purple-flushed stems with masses of small, purple flowers. It thrives in moist soil in part shade and may require staking in windy areas. H: 1.2m (4ft) S: 60cm (2ft). Hardiness 4 ☼ ☁

Thymus Thymes are dwarf, evergreen shrubs with fragrant leaves and clusters of small, pink or white flowers in summer. They thrive in dry soils in full sun. *T.* x *citriodorus* is a lemon-scented thyme with cream-edged leaves. H: 25cm (10in) S: 30cm (1ft). *T. doerfleri* 'Bressingham' has grey leaves and pink flowers. H: 10cm (4in) S: 30cm (1ft). *T. polytrichus* is a creeping shrub with dark green leaves and purple flowers. H: 5cm (2in) S: 60cm (2ft). *T. serpyllum* forms mats of green leaves and purple flowers. *T. vulgaris* is culinary thyme, a grey-leaved shrub with purple flowers. H: 12cm (1ft) S: 40cm (16in). Hardiness 4 ☼ ◊ ⊛ ✿ ☧ - spring

Tiarella cordifolia This creeping, herbaceous perennial forms effective ground cover in moist soil in semi-shade. The lobed, hairy leaves develop a brown tinge in late summer. In summer the spikes of small, white, fluffy flowers are produced. H: 25cm (10in) S: 60cm (2ft). Hardiness 4 ☁ ☁

Trachelospermum jasminoides

Tolmiea menziesii 'Taff's Gold' The unusual feature of this semi-evergreen, herbaceous perennial is that it forms young plants on its leaves and this is how it spreads rapidly as ground cover. This cultivar has gold-speckled foliage. The brownish, small, tubular flowers are produced on thin stems in summer. H: 45cm (18in) S: 60cm (2ft). Hardiness 4 ☁ ☁ ◊

Trachelospermum jasminoides This slightly frost-tender twining climber has dark evergreen leaves and requires a sheltered site. In summer the starry, white, fragrant flowers are produced in small clusters. H: 8m (25ft). Hardiness 3–4 ☼ ☁ ⊛ ☧ - spring

Trifolium pratense This perennial spreads rapidly with its creeping stems. The characteristic, three-lobed leaves are dotted with spherical heads of pink, fragrant flowers in summer. It is too vigorous for borders and should be restricted to the wild garden. H: 15cm (6in) S: 60cm (2ft). Hardiness 4 ☼ ◊ ✿

Trillium In the woodland garden, trilliums are colourful plants. They are rhizomatous, herbaceous, hardy perennials with erect stems and flowers in early summer. These have three petals and are held above three leaves, which are often mottled with purple. *T. grandiflorum* has pure white, large flowers. H: 40cm (16in) S: 30cm (1ft). *T. rivale* is dwarf with nodding, pink flowers. H: 12cm (5in) S: 15cm (6in). *T. sessile* has mottled leaves and deep red flowers. H: 30cm (1ft) S: 20cm (8in). Hardiness 4 ☁

Trollius The globe flowers are moisture-loving, hardy perennials that are suitable for poolside planting. They form clumps of coarsely divided leaves and in early summer produce their globular yellow or orange flowers. *T.* x *cultorum* 'Canary Bird' has pale yellow flowers. H: 75cm (30in) S: 45cm (18in). Hardiness 4 ☼ ☁ ◆

Tropaeolum majus The common nasturtium is an annual that thrives in dry or ordinary garden soil. The bright flowers are carried on mounded plants of blue-green, round leaves in summer. The flowers and leaves are edible and have a peppery taste. Hardiness 3 ☼ ◊

Tulipa 'Purissima' This Fosteriana hybrid has large flowers in spring that are cream in bud but open to pure white. Like most tulips it thrives in well-drained soil in full sun. *T.* 'Madame Lefeber' is similar but pure red. H: 35cm (14in) S: 10cm (4in). Hardiness 4 ☼

Typha minima The common reedmace or bulrush (*T. latifolia*) is too vigorous for garden ponds but this miniature species is rarely a nuisance. The slender leaves are joined, in late summer, by small spikes of brown flowers. It will grow in moist soil or shallow water. H: 75cm (30in) S: 30cm (1ft). Hardiness 4 ☼

Uvularia grandiflora The nodding, slender, yellow bells of this woodland plant open in early summer on arching stems of green leaves. It is a rhizomatous perennial that prefers rich, moist but well-drained soil. H: 60cm (2ft) S: 30cm (1ft). Hardiness 4 ☁

Vaccinium vitis-idaea The cowberry is a spreading, dwarf, evergreen shrub with small, round, glossy green leaves. The nodding pink or white flowers are produced in early summer and these are followed by edible red berries. It requires moist, acid soil. H: 25cm (10in) S: 60cm (2ft). Hardiness 4 ☼ ☁ ☧

Valeriana phu 'Aurea' This herbaceous perennial forms clumps of deeply cut leaves and in summer it has tall stems of small, pink or white flowers. The foliage is bright yellow when it first emerges in spring, but by flowering time this has changed to green. H: 1.2m (4ft) S: 60cm (2ft). Hardiness 4 ☼ ☁

Verbascum Most verbascums have tall spikes of yellow flowers and are herbaceous perennials or biennials, but a few are dwarf shrubs for dry soil and rock gardens. *V. bombyciferum* is a biennial that forms a rosette of large, silver-haired leaves in the first year followed by 'candelabra' stems of yellow flowers. H: 2.5m (8ft) S: 60cm (2ft). *V.* 'Letitia' is a dwarf shrub for dry soil with small grey leaves and bright yellow flowers in summer. H: 25cm (10in) S: 30cm (1ft). *V. olympicum* is a monocarpic perennial with branched spikes of yellow flowers. H: 2m

Uvularia grandiflora

Weigela florida 'Foliis Purpureis'

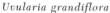

(6ft) S: 60cm (2ft). Hardiness 4

Verbena These are slightly tender or tender annuals and perennials, although in the garden most are treated as bedding plants. They are grown for their clusters of small, bright flowers. *V. bonariensis* is a hardy herbaceous perennial with thin, stiffly upright stems and small heads of purple flowers in summer. H: 2m (6ft) S: 45cm (18in). *V.* x *hybrida* is a spreading, hairy-leaved perennial usually treated as a half-hardy annual raised from seed. 'Amethyst' has purple flowers and Derby and Tropic are mixtures. H: 25cm (10in) S: 30cm (1ft). V. 'Lawrence Johnston' is a spreading perennial with bright red flowers. H: 45cm (18in) S: 60cm (2ft). *V. rigida* is a tuberous perennial, treated as an annual with angular-branched stems and purple flowers. H: 45cm (18in) S: 40cm (16in). V. 'Silver Anne' has scented, pink flowers that fade to pale pink. H: 30cm (1ft) S: 60cm (2ft). V. 'Sissinghurst' has strident pink flowers and grey leaves. H: 20cm (8in) S: 1m (3ft). Hardiness 3–4

Veronica beccabunga This pondside perennial has creeping stems and pairs of evergreen, round leaves. In summer it has short spikes of pale blue flowers. It will grow in moist soil or shallow water. H: 10cm (4in) S: 60cm (2ft). Hardiness 4

Viburnum rhytidophyllum This hardy evergreen shrub has pairs of long, wrinkled, leathery leaves and clusters of white flowers in late spring, sometimes followed by red, then black, berries. H: 5m (16in) S: 3m (10ft). Hardiness 4 - spring

Vicia cracca Tufted vetch is a perennial that has showy spikes of violet flowers above the ferny leaves in summer. It should only be grown in wild gardens. H: 45cm (18in) S: 45cm (18in). Hardiness 4

Vinca minor The lesser periwinkle is a useful evergreen ground-cover shrub, with creeping stems and dark green leaves. The blue, starry flowers are produced in summer. f. *alba* has white flowers. 'Atropurpurea' has wine-red flowers. 'Argenteovariegata' has white-edged leaves and blue flowers. H: 15cm (6in) S: 1m (3ft). Hardiness 4

Viola This genus includes sweet violets, pansies and violas. Most do best in moist, well-drained soil and are hardy, herbaceous perennials grown for their flowers in winter or late spring. *V.* x *wittrockiana* is the pansy, usually grown from seed and treated as an annual or biennial. V. 'Ardross Gem' has blue and yellow flowers. V. 'Belmont Blue' has small blue flowers. *V. cornuta* is the tufted viola, with long-spurred, blue flowers; 'Minor' is more compact with smaller flowers. *V.* 'Jersey Gem' has purple flowers. *V. odorata* 'Alba' has snow white, scented flowers. *V. riviniana* Purpurea Group has purple leaves and violet flowers. *V. tricolor* is the wild viola with cream and purple flowers. H: 15cm (6in) S: 30cm (1ft). Hardiness 4

Vitis vinifera 'Purpurea' A purple-leaved cultivar of the common wine grape, this plant climbs by tendrils. Its leaves turn scarlet and crimson in autumn. It is a hardy, woody climber for a sheltered part of the garden. H: 7m (22ft). Hardiness 4 - winter

Weigela florida 'Foliis Purpureis' This hardy, deciduous shrub has bronze leaves, and deep pink flowers in early summer. For best colour, grow in full sun. The plants should be pruned after flowering. H: 1m (3ft) S: 1.5m (5ft). Hardiness 4 - after flowering

Yucca These exotic evergreen perennials have rosettes of spiny, narrow leaves and spires of bell-shaped, waxy, white flowers in summer. They withstand drought and are most hardy when planted in sun and dry soil. *Y. filamentosa* is a small species with thin-textured leaves edged with curly hairs, 'Variegata' has leaves edged in white. H: 75cm (30in) S: 1.5m (5ft). *Y. gloriosa* has a stout trunk and stiff, sharp-tipped leaves. H: 2m (6ft) S: 2m (6ft). Hardiness 3–4

Zantedeschia aethiopica This lush perennial is slightly tender and in cold areas should be grown in pots, mulched in winter, or planted in water with the crown below the freeze zone. It will grow in moist soil, at pond edges or in water. The large, white, 'arum' flowers are borne above the arrowhead-shaped leaves in early summer. H: 1m (3ft) S: 60cm (2ft). Hardiness 3–4

Zauschneria californica The Californian fuchsia is a grey-leaved, small shrub that thrives in dry soil in full sun. It is a useful addition to the rock garden because the bright scarlet flowers are produced in late summer when most alpines are looking tired. It is hardy in dry, sheltered sites. H: 30cm (1ft) S: 50cm (20in). Hardiness 4

INDEX

ACKNOWLEDGMENTS

The publisher thanks the following illustrators for their kind permission to reproduce the illustrations in this book: **12–13, 18–19, 20, 24, 31, 32, 34, 52, 53, 68, 69, 72, 73, 80–1, 82–3, 84–5, 86–7, 92, 94, 96, 100–1, 112, 114, 115, 116–7, 118–19, 121–1** Shirley Felts; **14, 16, 25, 36, 74, 98** Fiona Bell-Currie; **22, 26, 38–9, 70, 78, 88–9** Jeremy Ford; **29, 42, 445, 45, 46, 48, 50, 56, 58, 60, 61, 62, 76, 77, 102, 104, 106, 108, 122, 123** Lynn Chadwick.

The publisher thanks the following photographers and organizations for their kind permission to reproduce the photographs in this book: **1** Andrew Lawson; **2–3** Marianne Majerus (Designer: Will Giles); **4–5** Marianne Majerus (Bennington Lordship); **6–7** Andrew Lawson; **8** and **9** S & O Mathews; **10–11** S & O Mathews (Clare College, Cambridge); **40** S & O Mathews; **54–55** Jo Whitworth; **66** Jerry Harpur (Tessa King-Farlow); **90–91** Andrew Lawson; **110–111** Marianne Majerus (Whichford Pottery); **125** *left and right* Andrew Lawson; **125** *centre* and **126** Jo Whitworth; **127** *left and right* Andrew Lawson; **128** *left* Jo Whitworth; **128** *right*, **129**, **130** and **131** *left* Andrew Lawson; **131 right** Howard Rice; **132** and **133** *left* Jo Whitworth; **133** *right*, **134** *left*, **134** *right* and **135** Andrew Lawson; **136** Howard Rice; **137** *left* Jo Whitworth; **137** *right* Howard Rice; **138** *left* Andrew Lawson; **138** *right* Howard Rice; **139** and **140** Andrew Lawson; **141** *left and right* Howard Rice; **142** *left* Jo Whitworth; **142** *right* and **143** Andrew Lawson; **144** Howard Rice; **145** *left and right* Andrew Lawson; **146** *left*, **146** *right* and **147** Jo Whitworth; **148** Andrew Lawson; **149** *left* Jo Whitworth; **149** *right*, **150** *left and right*, **151** and **152** Andrew Lawson; **153** *left* Howard Rice; **153** *right*, **154**, **155** *left and right* Andrew Lawson.